The Mischief of Sin
Recapturing the Stigma of Sin in Preaching

Pure Water Press

The Mischief of Sin
Recapturing the Stigma of Sin in Preaching

This book is dedicated to my wife, Lori.
The words of Solomon suffice the explanation,
"Her children rise up and call her blessed;
her husband also, and he praises her."

Timothy P. Juhnke
Kansas City, Missouri
May 2012

 Pure Water Press is committed to publishing books and materials that proclaim the gospel of Jesus Christ and the sufficiency of the Scriptures.

Copyright © 2014 by Timothy Juhnke.
All Rights Reserved

ISBN# **978-0692284896**

Unless otherwise indicated, all Scripture quotations are from *The Holy Bible, English Standard Version*® (ESV®), copyright © 2001 by Crossway, a publishing ministry of Good News Publishers. Used by permission. All rights reserved.

Table of Contents

Preface 5
Introduction Christianity and Sin 9
Chapter One - The Language of Sin 23
Chapter Two - Culture and Sin 39
Chapter Three - The Sinfulness of Sin 55
Chapter Four - The Mind and Sin 71
Chapter Five - Self-Righteousness and Sin 85
Chapter Six - The Will and Sin 99
Chapter Seven - The Body and Sin 113
Chapter Eight - Relationships and Sin 135
Conclusion - The Gospel and Sin 149
Bibliography 169

Author's Note:

In 1671 Thomas Watson first published *The Mischief of Sin.* Originally, it was a discourse to his family that he made available to the public. His prayer for his readers was that God would make the work "operative on your heart." It was operative on mine; and it was the inspiration for the present book. A lot has changed over 300 years plus, but one thing has not - the mischief of sin.

Preface

Since the subject of sin is prevalent and predominant throughout Scripture, it has always been integral to the Christian faith and message. While many may still associate Christians as being against sin, mainstream Christianity has undergone profound changes on the subject. The language of sin is being jettisoned in favor of psychological labels like "compulsions" and "dysfunctions" that ultimately lessen the stigma of the evildoer. Moreover, there are significant attempts today to root the effects of sin like depression, anxiety, anger, and guilt into biological abnormalities rather than in human depravity. Losing the concept of sin will ultimately marginalize the role of the church and, especially, the role of preaching in society.

Throughout the history of redemption, God has employed the office of prophet to confront His people in their sin and call them to repentance. In the New Covenant, as ministers of the gospel, the Christian preacher has the responsibility to retain the language of sin and to situate man's ultimate problem in his rebellion and alienation from his Creator.

In examining the comprehensive nature of sin, five aspects of sin are examined that are specific to the role of preaching: the integral relationship of sin to the Christian faith (introduction), significant forces operative in jettisoning the language of sin from the pulpit (chapters 1-2), a recovery of the sinfulness of sin (chapter 3), the comprehensive effects of sin on the person (chapters 4-8), and the unique way that the gospel alone addresses the problem of sin (conclusion). Each of these aspects is discussed at length. Throughout each of these chapters, these aspects of sin are specifically examined in the light of preaching and the preacher's responsibility. In each chapter, practical applications are interspersed throughout to aid the preacher in implementing a preaching ministry that retains a focus on the problem of sin.

When the comprehensive importance of sin is recovered in a preaching ministry, the role of preaching takes on a whole new level of significance. Anemic sermons that only address superficial needs will be rejected. *The Mischief of Sin* seeks to inspire in a new generation of preachers a courage to call sin what it is and to recover a new found confidence in the gospel, which is the only remedy to man's sick condition.

The truth is that without the problem of sin we do not need the gospel.
Page 11

Introduction: Christianity and Sin

Reconciling and balancing a checkbook is a necessary evil of life. It seems that even when you try to keep a good record of your spending, there are always expenses that you forget to record. I do not know why our mistakes always tend to subtract from the bottom line and never add to it, but they do. In the past I have put off reconciliation for months, but in the end it only makes matters worse. Another approach one could adopt is the method of one of my friends who simply never reconciled his statements. At times I am not even sure he opened the envelopes. It probably saves some stress in the short term, but it is definitely not recommended for long term financial stability. Sooner or later you have to face the facts. Ignorance can be bliss for a while, but eventually reality catches up with you.

The reluctance we might experience opening a bank statement or credit card bill pales in comparison to the general unwillingness that we have in opening up the book of our life. Personal accounting is much harder to face. As Harvard psychiatrist Dr. Armand Nicholi put it, "Within the university, students and professors scrutinize every possible aspect of our universe—from the billions of galaxies to subatomic particles, electrons, quarks—but they assiduously avoid examining their own lives."[1] This is not just a problem among the academic elite; it is one of America's pastimes. I am convinced that endless amusements, constant stimulations, relentless noise, and generally hectic lives are perpetually employed to fill the emptiness and avoid the shame that exists deep within our soul. When it comes to a personal reckoning, we will chase every possible distraction to avoid facing these uncomfortable truths.

The uncomfortable truths we prefer to keep hidden are often a litany of failures that litter our past, like stupid decisions, irresponsibility, hypocrisy, reckless relationships, and generally inept behaviors. Ironically, the Bible has one little word that encompasses them all—sin. It is the exposure of our sin that we assiduously avoid, and we will go to great lengths to conceal it. Incredibly, the world in which we live

---

[1] Armand M. Nicholi, *The Question of God* (New York: Free Press, 2002), 6.

has become a ready accomplice to our schemes. Many of the voices that once might have called us out (like parents, pastors, educators, and even medical practitioners) have been muted; some have even become our co-conspirators. These spin doctors help us employ sophisticated measures that redefine the failures that haunt our lives.

If there is one voice that should be faithful in telling the truth, it is the Church. This book is written to encourage the Christian preacher to recapture in his preaching the stigma of sin to a generation in which sin abounds but truth about sin does not. David Tyler and Kurt Grady, in their book, *Deceptive Diagnosis,* make the obvious point that "Christianity does not make sense without sin."[2] As a minister of the Word, the preacher has a divinely appointed task of reconciling the world to God, and this prophetic office of reconciliation always involves an honest accounting of one's sin. Failures have to be exposed—people have to know where they really stand before God—before the remedy can be applied. The ministry of reconciliation, however, can be a dangerous business because honest accounting is painful. In fact, Israel had a nasty habit of mocking and killing the divine messengers who called them to repent.[3]

Superficial Remedies

Nobody likes to be mocked or killed, so it is not surprising that many of Israel's prophets timidly shirked their responsibility. When the people of Israel faced impending judgment because of their rebellion against God, their religious leaders applied solutions that ignored the real problem. It made the people feel better, but without repentance the dismal consequences of their rebellion was inevitable. Their failure was palpable. Through the prophet Jeremiah, the Lord declared, "They have healed the brokenness of My people superficially, saying, 'Peace, peace,' when there is no peace" (Jer 6:14).[4] Referring to these false prophets, D.A. Carson wrote, "There is nothing in their preaching

---

[2] David Tyler and Kurt Grady. *Deceptive Diagnosis* (Bemidji, MN: Focus Publishing, 2006), 14.

[3] See 1 Kings 19:14; Neh 9:26; 2 Chron 36:17; Acts 7:52; Rom 11:3; 1 Thess 2:15.

[4] All Scripture references are from the ESV unless otherwise noted.

which fosters poverty of spirit, nothing which searches the conscience and makes men cry to God for mercy…"[5]

Brokenness is an appropriate metaphor for the destructive nature of sin—broken homes, broken relationships, broken promises, and even broken hearts. The only thing which seemed unbroken in Israel was their pride, the stubborn refusal to recognize their rebellion against God. Israel and her prophets refused to see the correlation between their brokenness and sin. In fact, as the next verse records, they continued to sin boldly. "No," said the Lord, "they were not ashamed at all; they did not know how to blush" (Jer 6:15). In prescribing superficial remedies, the prophets misdiagnosed the brokenness of the people. John Stott wrote, "Superficial remedies are always due to a faulty diagnosis. Those who prescribe them have fallen victim to the deceiving spirit of modernity which denies the gravity of sin."[6]

The "deceiving spirit" of modernity was operative in Israel and it is clearly alive and well in our postmodern age. Denying the gravity of sin is endemic to human nature. The ruins of brokenness are all around us. We see it in our government, in the judicial system, in our schools, in our families, and in our churches. At the same time we see purveyors of peace running to and fro trying to fix the brokenness; yet, there remains in our collective society an entrenched aversion to connect the brokenness to sin. As ministers in the New Covenant, preachers have a prophetic responsibility to expose the inherent problem of sin.

I have no illusions that a book about sin will become a best seller. It is not a popular subject today. As a pastor, you might think that I have a vested interest in the subject of sin. If sin did not exist we would not need pastors, but this is not a book about how pastors can keep their jobs. The truth is that without the problem of sin we do not need the gospel. Ultimately, the subject of sin concerns the heart and soul of the Christian faith. It is not a peripheral issue. It answers some of the deepest and most basic questions of our faith, questions like: What is the gospel? What is the Christian life all about? Various answers to

---

[5] D.A. Carson, *Jesus' Sermon on the Mount and His Confrontation with the World* (Grand Rapids: BakerBooks, 1987), 135.
[6] John Stott, *The Cross of Christ* (Downers Grove, IL: InterVarsity Press, 1986), 99.

these questions are emerging that bear little resemblance to the biblical testimony.

We have witnessed a significant section of Christendom that has propagated a very popular alteration of the Christian life into something about wealth and prosperity. This movement has essentially prostituted the gospel for the sake of greed and crass materialism, as if we are supposed to have our best life now. We have been told that an abundant life is ours for the taking if we will only "name and claim it" in faith. If you watch late night Christian programming on TV, you will be bombarded with ministries promising an abundant "harvest" if you will just "seed" their ministry with a generous donation. These ministries also often claim that physical healing is promised by the suffering of Jesus if only enough faith will be exercised. This "health and wealth" gospel has been rightly rejected by evangelicals, but the questions remain: What did the gospel accomplish for us? What is the Christian life all about?

Scripture is not ambiguous about these answers. The gospel offers to us nothing less than eternal life through the forgiveness of sins. Does that shock you? Were you expecting something more? If we look for something greater out of the gospel than the forgiveness of sin, we exhibit a profound misunderstanding of how desperate our condition really is before God. Before our reconciliation by the gospel we were *enemies* of God (Rom 5:10). Our greatest problem was that our sin stood against us and cried out for His righteous wrath. It is the existence of sin that wreaks havoc in our lives, in the world, in our family, and in the Church. This is the problem the gospel addresses. The gospel reconciles us to God so completely that neither tribulation, nor distress, nor persecution, nor famine, nor nakedness, nor danger, nor sword can separate us from His love (Rom 8:32–37). Paraphrasing Paul, "If God is for us, who cares who is against us?" (Rom 8:31).

It is the Church, the Body of Christ, which bears the responsibility of offering the peace terms of the gospel to a world alienated from God (2 Cor 5:18–20). As overseers of the church, pastors ultimately shape this message. As long as the problem of sin is obscured, the pastoral ministry will be greatly marginalized, if not outright irrelevant. This is becoming more of a reality than we realize. As the concept of sin has been greatly diminished, the maladies of sin have been increasingly relegated over to secular psychiatry, and increasingly more common, to medical professionals.

The purpose of this book is to call pastors back to their God-given role of addressing humanity's inherent problem that permeates every area of life. Understanding the "disease" of sin, exposing it, and treating it will require a boldness that has become increasingly uncommon in the pulpit today. If preachers do not address the reality and problem of sin, they ultimately fail in their obligations as true ministers of the soul. If the problem of sin is ever going to be recovered, we can be sure that it will not come from sociologists, psychologists, or politicians. It can only come from the church.

Only by understanding the comprehensive nature of sin will the Church and the world really see how malignant the disease of sin is. Unfortunately, today when people are faced with maladies of sin, they are more prone to consult a psychiatrist or doctor than a preacher. Tragically, we see misery, suffering, and destruction all around us; but what is even more tragic is the unwillingness even among preachers to acknowledge the real root cause of all these problems. Man by nature is programmed to find reasons for consequences and behaviors that remove personal responsibility. Unfortunately, the growing tendency in the pulpit is to accommodate the gospel to needs that are perceived to be more pressing than the problem of sin. Apart from addressing the stigma of sin, these attempts are tantamount to proclaiming "peace" when there is no peace; and without true repentance, the destructive maladies of sin are inevitable and inescapable.

The modern pulpit has a penchant for relevance. Of course, any preacher worth his salt must be relevant; but the quest for relevance has too often resulted in the abandonment of the biblical message in favor of pick-me-up sermonettes that fail to address the most malignant problem facing the human race. The misplaced attempts to be relevant have ironically resulted in the church becoming one of the most irrelevant institutions in our country. This is most evident when we see disturbed people with real emotional and psychological problems routinely outsourced to "professional" care outside of the Church. What kind of message does that send to the world? What kind of message does that send to believers? Bringing people face to face with the reality of sin and its destructive consequences is the only true holistic approach to ministry. The gospel message is inherently relevant because sin affects and touches every area of our life. In the following chapters we will examine just how thoroughly sin poisons every aspect of our existence.

The epistles of the New Testament abound with exhortations to guard the deposit of truth.[7] The apostle Jude goes so far as to say *contend* or fight for the faith that was *once for all delivered to the saints* (Jude 1:3). These exhortations reveal a premium on doctrinal integrity within the local church and the need to preserve the faith as it was once delivered. As an organic institution constantly faced with threats from false teaching, the Church does not trend toward orthodoxy. According to Jude, it must be maintained with vigilance. Our faith is not only in danger of being hijacked by false teachers, but we face the often subtle and imperceptible risk of drifting away from the truth. As the author of Hebrews warned, "…We must pay much closer attention to what we heard, lest we drift from it" (Heb 2:1). As we survey the brokenness around us, we intuitively see that we are a culture in moral, economic, and spiritual decline. Purveyors of peace are calling for "change." Some assume that change requires something new or novel; but in a culture of decline, the standard we aspire to is in the past. In the church there are similar calls for change. Some are suggesting we need new methods to recover our glory. Perhaps more than ever, however, maybe we need to consider from where we came.

Lessons from the Pages of History

One of the great slogans of the Protestant reformation was *semper reformanda*—always reforming. The Church must be diligent to constantly evaluate and reform its doctrines and practices and traditions back to the standard of Scripture. The rallying cry of Martin Luther, one of the leading architects of the Protestant Reformation, was *sola Scriptura*—Scripture alone as the standard and guide of the Church. In the succeeding generations it was the Puritans who carried that torch, and they have passed this great heritage down to us. We have voluminous records of their sermons and books. Sure, it takes a little time to get accustomed to their imposing vocabulary, but when you wade through their works they evidence a profound grasp of Scripture. Almost four centuries later, their expositions still resonate

---

[7] 2 Thess 2:15; 1 Tim 6:20; 2 Tim 1:13–4, 3:14; Titus 1:9.

with a relevancy that poignantly illustrates that the Word of God is truly living and active.

A number of Christians today would credit the Puritans for the revival of faith and practice in their own walk. Sadly, too many people only think of the Puritans as dour, boring, judgmental killjoys who burned witches at Salem. Our forefathers had their problems for sure. They were not perfect or infallible, but their vibrant, experiential faith still speaks loudly today. I credit these godly men with provoking within me a fresh look on the subject of sin. I am convinced that in this generation the need for reformation is dire. I am thankful that the Puritans have awakened in me the biblical standard that is quite foreign to what many have become accustomed to today. Without their example, I wonder if the church today would ever realize just how far we have drifted from the revelation of God's Word.

Sin was a popular subject among the Puritans because it is such a prominent subject in Scripture. The truth is that the Puritans preached against sin and *about* sin much more than we contemporaries do. That is probably one of the reasons they are often thought of as killjoys. Their emphasis upon sin is really what makes their version of Christianity so much different than the one prevailing today. One of the oldest Puritan books I read was *Evil of Evils, or the Exceeding Sinfulness of Sin* by Jeremiah Burroughs first published in 1654.[8] Interestingly, John Yates, the man who penned the original foreword in *Evil of Evils,* wrote, "And though various divines have written and spoken much concerning this subject, yet in my poor judgment, this out-does all of this nature that ever my eyes beheld…"[9] This statement seems to clearly indicate that in that particular age the subject of sin proliferated in books and sermons. However, Yates believed that under the gospel light of free grace, many professing believers had become lackadaisical in their attitude toward sin. He wrote, "I am persuaded that more men drop down to hell in our day under the abuse of gospel light than ever did in the gross darkness of popery."[10] The careless attitude toward sin that flourished in the church compelled Burroughs to compose *The Evil of Evils,* and he had one unrelenting premise:

---

[8] Jeremiah Burroughs, *Evil of Evils or The Exceeding Sinfulness of Sin* (1654; repr.., Ligonier, PA: Soli Deo Gloria, 1992).
[9] Ibid., xvi.
[10] Burroughs, *Evil of Evils,* xvii.

"My principal business is to charge men's consciences with the evil of their sin and show to them how much evil there is in sin."[11]

Burroughs was not an anomaly. The Puritan focus on sin was unrelenting. Just a few years later Ralph Venning published the book *The Sinfulness of Sin*.[12] It is one of the most thorough treatments on the subject of sin that I have ever encountered. His intent was to dwell upon the "malignity and wicked nature of sinful sin."[13] Expounding upon that purpose he wrote,

> If we look on [sin] through the microscope-glass of the law, it will appear a most hideous, devilish and hellish thing, the most wicked, mischievous, virulent, villainous and deadly thing that ever was. Sinful sin! Worse than the Devil![14]

That is a lot of superlatives and adjectives to pile together in one sentence, but I think he made his point.

A few years later, in 1671 another influential Puritan, Thomas Watson, wrote *The Mischief of Sin*.[15] [It was Watson's work that first convicted me to address this issue.] "Mischief" may not sound so bad. It seems more innocent than evil—maybe innocence only tinged with evil. English words, however, change over the years, and the word mischief is one of them. Today, we might define mischief as some type of petty, playful foolishness, but if we want to capture Watson's meaning of mischief we would need to consult a dictionary a little closer in time to the source—the 1828 Webster's original dictionary. It defined mischief as "harm; hurt; intentional injury; ill consequence."[16] That was what Watson meant when he wrote about the "mischief" of sin. He expounded upon the devastating effects that sin has upon people— the brokenness that sin begets. As Watson put it, "Sin first brings us

---

[11] Ibid., 2.
[12] This work was originally published as *The Plague of Plagues* in 1669.
[13] Ralph Venning, *The Sinfulness of Sin* (1669; repr,; Carlisle, PA: Banner of Truth, 1993), 29.
[14] Ibid., 21.
[15] Thomas Watson, *The Mischief of Sin* (1671; repr., Morgan, PA: Soli Deo Gloria Publications, 1994).
[16] http://1828.mshaffer.com/d/word/mischief (accessed 5/4/2012).

pleasures which delight and charm the senses, and then comes the nail and hammer…Sin's last act is always tragic."[17]

Let me indulge in just one more example. A few years after *The Mischief of Sin* was published, another Puritan, Thomas Boston, penned another discourse on sin titled *Human Nature in Its Fourfold State of Primitive Integrity, Entire Depravity, and Consummate Happiness or Misery* [the Puritans did not share our penchant for short, pithy titles]. It is one of the religious classics that came out of Scotland in the early 18th century. In *Human Nature in Its Fourfold State,* Boston painstakingly described how thoroughly sin has infected the human soul in its state of depravity. In confirming the doctrine of the corruption of human nature, Boston wrote, "I shall hold the glass to your eyes, wherein you may see your sinful nature; which, though God takes particular notice of it, many quite overlook."[18] For well over a century in all these works we see the theme of the sinfulness of sin as a constant refrain.

There is no doubt that the Puritans preached and wrote much against sin. One of the most famous sermons ever preached in America, "Sinners in the Hands of an Angry God," was delivered on July 8, 1741 by Jonathan Edwards. His portrayal of impending judgment on the wicked is so shocking in places that it would almost certainly be censored in many pulpits across America today. For instance, Edwards preached,

> God is holding you over the pit of hell, as someone who holds a spider or some repulsive insect over a fire, and He abhors you and is dreadfully provoked. His wrath toward you burns like fire, and He sees you as worthy of nothing else but to be thrown into that fire. His eyes are too pure even to look at you; you are ten thousand times more detestable in His sight than the most hated poisonous snake is in ours. You have offended Him infinitely more

---

[17] Watson, *The Mischief of Sin*, 21.
[18] Thomas Boston, *Human Nature in its Fourfold State,* http://www.gracegems.org/28/human_nature.htm (accessed 3/11/2011).

than even a stubborn rebel did his prince.et, it is nothing but God's hand that holds you from falling into the fire every moment.[19]

This kind of preaching illustrates just how much has changed in the church today. For most Christians today, Edwards's words would be as offensive as they are shocking. Frankly, we cannot even conceive of telling people that God abhors them, that they are worthy of nothing else but to be thrown into the fire, or that they are ten thousand times more detestable in His sight than the most poisonous snake is in ours. This sermon not only demonstrates how intensely the Puritans viewed the corrupting influence of sin on the human heart, but how much has changed over the years. Some would relegate Edward's remarks to those of a deranged Puritan; but if the language of Scripture is still the standard, then God's verdict on sin has not changed, but our concept of it has.

In this generation the stigma of sin has undergone massive transformations. The problem of sin has been eclipsed by concerns perceived more pressing than sin, and this is true among pastors and congregations alike. Years ago, a sermon such as "Sinners in the Hands of an Angry God" would not be uncommon. Preaching was often associated with "hellfire and brimstone." Such preaching, however, is generally a relic of the past. Today, that kind of preaching might evoke more embarrassment than conviction. The doctrine of judgment and hell is not a prominent theme in sermons. Several years ago after I preached a series on hell, a woman told me that even though she had attended church most of her life, she had never heard a sermon on hell. Since Jesus spoke more about hell than any other person in Scripture, it seems logical that His faithful messengers must also address this solemn subject.

The doctrine of hell is again under serious attack today. Hell has never been a popular subject. Liberals have always castigated it, but today there are many purported "evangelicals" who aggressively attempt to undermine what the Bible teaches awaits those who reject Jesus Christ.

---

[19] John Jeffery Fanella, *Jonathan Edwards Sinners in the Hands of an Angry God, Made Easier to Read* (Phillipsburg, New Jersey: P&R Publishing, 1996), 18.

The most notable and recent attempt to undermine the doctrine of eternal torment comes from Rob Bell in his book *Love Wins*. Bell undermines the sentence of eternal condemnation by asserting that people in hell will have a chance to repent. He transforms hell into a reformatory rather than a place of eternal death. In essence, the judgment of hell is remedial not punitive. He writes, "Failure, we see again and again, isn't final, judgment has a point, and consequences are for correction."[20] He adds,

> Could God say to someone truly humbled, broken, and desperate for reconciliation, "Sorry, too late"? Many have refused to accept the scenario in which somebody is pounding on the door, apologizing, repenting, and asking God to be let in, only to hear God say through the keyhole: "Door's locked. Sorry. If you had been here earlier, I could have done something. But now it's too late."[21]

In describing the new heaven and earth, Bell extrapolates his semi-universalism from the fact that the New Jerusalem will have gates that never shut (Rev 21:25). He writes, "But gates, gates are for keeping people in and keeping people out. If the gates are never shut then people are free to come and go."[22] According to Bell, preaching the endless punishment of hell "isn't a very good story."[23] Sadly, many see Bell's book as revolutionary and innovative; but it is neither. He is merely a puppet of the culture, mimicking the sentiments that have been formulating and brewing for decades.

In light of the current culture, we can be sure that *Love Wins* will not be the last assault on the doctrine of hell. Some evangelicals argue persuasively that the doctrine of hell may well become a test for orthodoxy in our day. Albert Mohler has suggested that "the doctrine of hell serves very well as a test case for the slide into theological liberalism."[24] What we believe about hell ultimately becomes a barometer for what we believe about sin and the gospel. We must be

---

[20] Rob Bell, *Love Wins: A Book about Heaven, Hell, and the Fate of Every Person Who Ever Lived* (New York: HarperOne, 2011), 88.
[21] Ibid., 108.
[22] Bell, *Love Wins*, 115.
[23] Ibid., 110.
[24] Albert Mohler, "Air Conditioning Hell: How Liberalism Happens," http://www.albertmohler.com/2010/01/26/air-conditioning-hell-how-liberalism-happens/ (accessed 2/15/2012).

faithful to the revelation of Scripture and vigilantly guard against false teaching. I am thankful that a number of able pastors and scholars have already responded to these attacks on hell with careful expositions of Scripture.[25]

Proving the doctrine of eternal torment from the Scriptures, however, is only a partial answer. Bell reads the same Bible that you and I do. I am sure that he knows all the proof texts. There is a reason that hell is under fire today, and it is not because the Bible is ambiguous or unclear. People are revolted by the doctrine of hell because they do not grasp the sinfulness of sin. For people like Bell, hell is unjust and cruel. They cannot fathom eternal damnation because they do not see sin for what it is. We can argue all day long about the doctrine of hell from Scripture, but if you do not grasp evil as "sinful beyond measure" (Rom 7:13), then the divine judgment of everlasting punishment is on par with a judge who sentences a jaywalker to the electric chair—the punishment is far worse than the crime.

More than ever we need to realize that the preaching of judgment *against* sin can only be effective to the degree that the offense of sin is known. In essence, preaching *about* sin must precede preaching *against* sin. Understanding the nature of sin is a prerequisite to understanding its punishment. For the apostle Paul this necessitated the Law. He wrote in Romans 7:13, "It was sin, producing death in me through what was good, in order that sin might be shown to be sin, and through the commandment might become sinful beyond measure." Sin *has* to become sinful—beyond measure.

One of the interesting facts about the Puritan works that I listed above that shaped and influenced Jonathan Edwards, his famous sermon, and his listeners, was that they all understood the exceeding sinfulness of sin. They did not just preach against sin; they labored to show the wretched evil of sin. The Puritan emphasis upon the evils of sin permeated their preaching and writing, preparing the way for revival and the spread of the gospel. Their works show us not only how much our preaching has changed today, but also how desensitized people have become to the terrible realities of sin. It is more than apparent

---

[25] I highly recommend Francis Chan's *Erasing Hell: What God Said About Eternity and the Things We've Made Up* (Colorado Springs, CO: David C Cook, 2011).

that we live in a very different world. It seems that sin has disappeared and no one seems to have noticed.

Culturally speaking, one of the most significant elements to any preaching ministry today is a careful and consistent exposition of Scripture that recaptures the devastating problem of sin which confronts all of humanity. The natural trajectory of human nature is to minimize, rationalize, or blatantly ignore the sinfulness of sin. In the following pages we will look at just how much "mischief" sin causes in our life.

As spiritual iniquities are transformed into psychological complexities, the church is obviously ill-equipped and becomes increasingly irrelevant in the world.
Page 32

Chapter One - The Language of Sin

The pop-Christianity that has emerged over the last several decades stands in stark contrast to our Puritan heritage. Walk into a typical Christian bookstore today and you will not find many, if any, contemporary titles about sin—certainly not any bestsellers. If somebody ventured into a Christian bookstore to investigate what this whole Christianity thing is about, the stain of sin would be barely visible. In fact in the broader culture, it would seem that there are very few taboos left; not much is sacred any more. Merriam-Webster defines a taboo as something "banned on grounds of morality or taste."[26] Ironically, if there is a remaining taboo in our society, it would be the notion of sin itself.

It has become socially unacceptable to pass moral judgments upon others. The calling out of a person or behavior as "sinful" has become intolerable. The exertion of a moral standard over another is ranked right alongside deplorable behaviors like bigotry or racism. As moral relativism has taken root in the very fabric of our society, the concept of sin has been redefined and all but eradicated from our vocabulary. We are more likely to hear about a "dysfunctional" life rather than a sinful life. A couple living together before marriage were once "fornicators," now they are just "friends with benefits." "Homosexuality" has become an "alternative lifestyle." "Drunkenness" has been replaced by the "disease of alcoholism." "Addiction" is a much more suitable label than "bondage to iniquity," and "recovery from addictions" sounds much better than "repentance from sin." Behaviors once deemed idolatrous and sinful are now categorized as "co-dependency" or "chemical imbalances." With all these new terms, it seems that sinners are still sensitive to the labels that are put upon their sin. As Venning wrote, "Sinners dare not commit sin until they have given it a new name."[27]

---

[26] http://www.merriam-webster.com/dictionary/taboo (accessed 4/2/2012).
[27] Venning, *The Sinfulness of Sin*, 129.

Redefining Sin

The redefinition of sin seems to have worked. Stott wrote, "The very word 'sin' has in recent years dropped from most people's voices."[28] While the removal of sin from our culture is a *fait de complete*—a done deal—the process has been going on for decades. Almost forty years ago, psychiatrist Karl Menninger noted the disappearance of the concept of sin. In his book *Whatever Became of Sin?* he wrote, "It was a word once in everyone's mind, but is now rarely if ever heard. Does that mean that no sin is involved in our troubles...? Has no one committed any sins? Where, indeed, did sin go? What became of it?"[29] The fact is that our collective society has eschewed the concept of sin. It is a subject we are no longer willing to broach. Public educators cannot talk about it, and it is certainly not something politicians want to address. Even though we have become accustomed to the familiar banter of "family values" in political discourses, these noble slogans are really nothing more than sentimental notions of political correctness. You cannot have family values without morality, and there is no morality without the concept of sin. The real scandal, however, is not that the notion of sin has disappeared from the general public. The scandal is that the language of sin has all but vanished from the Church itself.

It seems that we have become too sophisticated for sin. Sin seems to have gone the way of demon possession. Liberal scholars have long asserted that the Gospel writers did not understand the problems of mental illnesses and diseases, so they just blamed all these terrible maladies on demons. Sin has met the same fate. Many Christians would probably never admit it, but in practice they view the Bible as overly simplistic. Although the Bible clearly and constantly situates our premiere problem in sin, it is presumed that our troubles are much more complicated than just rebellion against God.

---

[28] Stott, *The Cross of Christ*, 89.
[29] Karl Menninger, *Whatever Became of Sin?* (Westerleigh, UK: Hawthorn Books, 1973), 13.

Redefining the concept of sin will have subtle ramifications for the Church, many of which are already being manifested. I know of numerous instances where pastors have farmed out "dysfunctional" church members to professional care because they did not feel equipped to help them. Emotionally troubled Christians have been conditioned to seek specialized care, and they are more likely to seek a psychiatrist or medical doctor rather than a pastor. One has to wonder if this generation will ever experience the grace of sitting under a Spirit-empowered pulpit that will expose the resident evil of the heart. Sadly, the growing likelihood is that they will not. Preaching and pastoral care are different today; and preaching that exposes and confronts sin is rare indeed. Unless there is a fundamental reformation that starts in the pulpits of this land, we will carry on superficially healing the brokenness of people saying, "Peace, peace" when there is no peace.

Perhaps more than ever before, we need to recapture the language of sin in the pulpit. Before we can do that, though, we need to see what led to the demise of sin and the birth of a new language in Christianity that is so prevalent today. More importantly, we need to understand why the pulpit is uniquely suited to expose the inherent sinfulness of the human heart, and that it is divinely ordained to be the means of grace and healing. A cultural insurrection has emerged that threatens the very existence of biblical Christianity in the Western hemisphere. For decades numerous forces from without and within have exerted enormous influence and pressure upon the pulpit. These influences have successfully shaped the modern pulpit and its message into a pattern quite foreign to Scripture. Ultimately, the convergence of these forces must be seen for what they are: enemies of the gospel.

We should not be surprised that many of those who undermine the truth and represent the most profound threat to our faith and practice often will come from *within* the church. The apostle Paul warned, "For such men are false apostles, deceitful workmen, disguising themselves as apostles of Christ, and no wonder, for even Satan disguises himself as an angel of light" (2 Cor 11:13–14). Our enemies are more often than not masquerading as our "friends." I am convinced that the emergence of secular psychology, the therapeutic model of preaching, and the seeker-sensitive church have converged to fundamentally alter, not only the problem of sin, but the solution to sin and the pivotal role that preaching has in it. When you add to this the influence of postmodernism (which is covered in the next chapter), these accumulated forces have created the "perfect storm" which has all but decimated the concept of sin from our evangelical vocabulary.

The Influence of Psychology

Very few Christians seem to understand the profound effect that secular psychology has had upon Christianity, sin, and the nature of preaching. It would be hard to find anything more instrumental in removing the ugliness of sin than modern psychology. Psychology is man's attempt to understand the mind of man and answer the problems that vex it. William James was the pioneer and father of the development of modern psychology in America. As Professor of Philosophy at Harvard, it was his *Principles of Psychology*[30] published in 1890 that garnered him immediate attention. It has been said that no man has had a greater influence on the development of psychology in America than he.[31] When he was asked what the chief desire in his work was, he replied, "To find a balm for the human soul."[32]

When the founding architect of psychology in America is on a quest to find healing and relief for the human soul, the challenge to the church and the gospel should be unmistakable. Unfortunately, many church leaders never perceived the rivalry. In fact, Charles Kemp noted that "the writings of James were widely read by the clergy" and "became the source of illustrations in many sermons."[33] No one seemed to notice that his "balm for the human soul" was a subtle attack on the gospel, which is the only true remedy for the human condition.

Today, Sigmund Freud is inextricably linked to psychology. Freud appears on the lists of the greatest physicians of our time. Freud's philosophy was avowedly atheistic. Armand Nicholi, a professor at

---

[30] http://psychclassics.yorku.ca/James/Principles/index.htm (accessed 4/2/2012).
[31] Charles Kemp, *Physicians of the Soul: A History of Pastoral Counseling* (New York: MacMillan, 1947), 70.
[32] Ibid., 71.
[33] Ibid.

Harvard and expert on Freud, asserts that Freud has played a significant role in the secularization of our culture. He wrote,

> In the seventeenth century people turned to the discoveries of astronomy to demonstrate what they considered the irreconcilable conflict between science and faith; in the eighteenth century to Newtonian physics; in the nineteenth century to Darwin; in the twentieth century and still today, Freud is the atheist's touchstone.[34]

Without question, psychology has attempted to become and do what only the gospel does and can be. Initially, psychology was considered a branch of philosophy, but in the early twentieth century psychology emerged as something more than just a philosophy, claiming to be a science in its own right.

This development had a profound effect upon religious thought. In fact, in 1927 Harrison Elliot, who was greatly interested in progressive educational theory and leaned toward a social gospel from a liberal religious perspective, wrote, "The fact is that the development of psychology has more bearing upon religion than any other scientific advances."[35] Kemp was just as emphatic stating, "More than any other factor or development since the Reformation, this [development of psychology] had a profound influence on the more thoughtful clergy and religious leaders."[36] Though largely forgotten today, these men make it clear that in its early stages psychology had enormous influence on the church. Massive paradigm shifts were being forged that fundamentally changed the language of sinful behaviors and attitudes away from a biblical framework.

In recent years, Tyler and Grady point out that with the emergence of psychology, "a major shift began in how evangelicals viewed and dealt

---

[34] Nicholi, *The Question of God*, 2–3.
[35] Harrison Elliot, *The Bearing of Psychology upon Religion* (New York: Association Press, 1927), 7.
[36] Kemp, *Physicians of the Souls*, 69.

with sin. The Church stopped calling sinful and deviant behavior 'sin' and started calling it 'sickness.'"[37] Such a change resulted in a new dichotomy for the church, a dichotomy that radically altered the ministry of the preacher and his ministry of preaching. Now, calling out sinful behavior has a caveat. What was once sinful, may, in fact, only be a disorder. Instead of a person being responsible to God for his actions, he might just be a victim who is sick. And the perennial plague of guilt that used to be associated with sinful behaviors has been quietly transformed into a condition commonly assumed to be poor self-esteem. In this bloodless revolution, the caretaking of sinners was quietly wrested from the church and placed squarely in the hands of psychological experts. Sadly, many seminaries that train men for the ministry have become accomplices to the revolution by requiring pastoral students to take classes permeated with psychology rather than theology.

As ministers of reconciliation we must recognize that ultimately secular psychology is the world's attempt to understand and fix man's problems without reference to, or recognition of, God's revealed standard of truth. Though unpopular to say so, the evidence is clear. In the ancient world of seafaring, the northern stars were an essential guide for navigation. While other stars' positions in the sky changed throughout the night, the positions of the northern stars remained essentially fixed. They were the dependable indicators of direction. For the Christian, the Bible is our North Star. Its position remains fixed, and it alone is essential for our navigation through life. That is what the Psalmist meant when he wrote, "Your word is a lamp to my feet and a light to my path" (Ps 119:105).

In the prevailing culture of evangelicalism today, we have taken our eyes off the North Star and it is leading us into an abyss. In essence, the world has created a different reference point with its own set of instructions through psychology. Although numerous attempts have been made to integrate the "science" of psychology with Christianity, most Christian psychotherapy is nothing more than a few Bible verses sprinkled over the foundational premises of psychology. The fact is

---

[37] Tyler and Grady, *Deceptive Diagnosis*, 2.

that the philosophies of psychology and the divine revelation of Scripture have radically different premises. In undermining the inherent sinfulness of humanity, psychology has made man a victim of his environment and has established self-esteem as a basic human need that is indispensable for emotional well-being. The mental health industry has succeeded in transforming man's perception of his true problem.

The church has always been threatened by false teaching; that is not new. Significant portions of the New Testament epistles are strategically designed to warn against the dangers of false teaching because such teaching threatens the very fabric of the Christian faith. Yet many Christians fail to recognize the false teaching inherent in secular psychology. Tyler and Grady suggest that as the ancient city of Troy opened its gates for the Greek's "gift" of the Trojan horse, modern evangelicalism has opened its gates to another Trojan horse. Their assessment of psychology's Trojan horse is sobering. They write,

> This horse is not a literal wooden horse filled with enemy soldiers, but is the teachings of modern psychology. The integration of modern psychology with the Bible is indeed one of the most challenging issues facing the Church today…The issue is whether today's Christians are mixing men's ideas with the Bible. Amazingly, most Christian leaders today who rightly cry so fervently against false teachings are saying little if anything about the subtle shifts in biblical interpretation that undermine the faith of millions. In many cases it reflects a lack of awareness and understanding of the teachings of psychology.[38]

At its most basic level, modern psychology seeks to understand and explain the mind of man; however, without God's perspective it will surely be incomplete and inadequate, if not downright distorted. As divine revelation, the Bible provides a unique and authoritative perspective on all of life. Our study of the mind is framed by the infallible revelation of our Creator. If we truly want to understand the

---

[38] Tyler and Grady, *Deceptive Diagnosis*, 50.

mind of man, we have to come to grips with what the Bible says about the reality of sin and its devastating effects upon the body and soul.

The Influence of Therapeutic Preaching

Psychology has had a profound influence upon the church's concept of sin and its preaching. Redefined problems require redefined solutions. In addressing the superficial problems of people, churches have adopted a therapeutic model of preaching that addresses people's perceived poor self-esteem and other "felt" needs. As one guru of this movement wrote, "The ground we have in common with unbelievers is not the Bible, but our common needs, hurts, and interests as human beings."[39] Since our society is full of dysfunctional (the new word for sinful) behaviors, broken relationships, and generally unhappy people these common needs are prominent topics in a typical pulpit. The sermon takes on a whole new character when preaching is directed towards these superficial problems. In order to address these needs, a therapeutic sermon uses the Bible to cull out practical principles that can be applied toward fixing marriages and families and generally finding more abundance and joy in life.

The Drama of Redemption

While the Bible is full of practical wisdom, such a philosophy of ministry is tantamount to prostitution. It uses the Bible for illicit purposes. First of all, it treats the Word of God like an all-you-can-eat dinner buffet where you can pick and choose what you want to eat. Such a treatment of Scripture ignores the one massive theme of redemption that runs from Genesis to Revelation. Sermons that cull out practical principles from this grand overarching theme usually miss the true drama of redemption: Sinners delivered from the power of sin and reconciled to a holy God. For example, if we fit the story of David and Goliath in the unfolding drama of redemption, it is not a story that shows us how we can go out and slay the giants in our life. Rather, it is a story about a people who were powerless against their

---

[39] Rick Warren, *The Purpose-Driven Church* (Grand Rapids: Zondervan Publishing, 1995), 295.

enemies, yet God raised up for them a deliverer. In the drama of redemption, instead of trying to be a David, we are the powerless people who need a David. And God has raised up our Deliverer, Jesus Christ.

Preaching the drama of redemption will always bring people to a point of weakness and need. It will evoke a crisis of identity as we are forced to see ourselves as God sees us and a crisis of decision as we are compelled to turn from our own ways and follow His. Preaching the drama of redemption requires us to keep our focus on the gospel of grace and its power in our life. Using the Bible for simple steps to successful living or better marriages trivializes not only the gospel but the whole Christian way of life.

Most people do not come to church expecting to be challenged in their thinking. If they do, they will too often be sorely disappointed. Instead, they get a pick-me-up sermon so they can feel better about their life. Preaching has been reduced to anemic sermonettes offering pious platitudes that are of little use to the real problems people face. In 2011 Barna Research published an article entitled "Six Reasons Young Christians Leave the Church." According to Barna, the second reason young Christians leave the church is because their "experience of Christianity is shallow."[40] Over one-third of the respondents said that "church is boring"[41] and almost one-fourth responded that "faith is not relevant to my career or interests."[42] I believe these statistics demonstrate that the younger generation has become bored with these trifles and has begun to look outside of the church for substance and meaning.

It is imperative that we understand that the biblical drama of redemption is not just an ancient story—it is *our* story. As Dietrich Bonhoeffer stated in his book *Life Together,* "We are torn out of our own existence and set down in the midst of the holy history of God on earth. There God dealt with us, and there He still deals with us, our

---

[40] http://www.barna.org/teens-next-gen-articles/528-six-reasons-young-christians-leave-church (accessed 4/2/2012).
[41] Ibid.
[42] Ibid.

needs and sins, in judgment and grace."[43] When disconnected from the drama of redemption, preaching becomes marginalized and the maladies of sin are increasingly relegated to secular psychiatry and to medical professionals. When the church is confronted with really messed up people—people with personality disorders, bipolarism, obsessive compulsive behaviors, uncontrolled anger, etc., —they are usually going to be referred to care outside of the church because we have been duped into thinking that we are not equipped to handle them.

As spiritual iniquities are transformed into psychological complexities, the church is obviously ill-equipped and becomes increasingly irrelevant in the world. Moreover, as Tyler and Grady state, "Discarding the language of sin weakens and softens the full impact of grace."[44] The role of the church, at least in Western civilization, is in real trouble. Unless preachers understand and are willing to address the *real* problem facing people, they becomes worthless to society. As Jesus said, salt that loses its saltiness "is no longer good for anything except to be thrown out and trampled under people's feet" (Matt 5:13).

A New Reformation?

Robert Schuller, former pastor of the Crystal Cathedral and guru of positive-thinking, epitomized the massive paradigm shift that results when the church tried to integrate secular psychology with biblical Christianity. Schuller believed that the church needed a new reformation—a new theological reformation. According to Schuller, the church had to accommodate the scientific development of psychology. He wrote, "A widespread tension has too long existed between psychologists and theologians. Both disciplines should be committed to the healing of the human spirit. Both can and must learn from each other."[45] He then audaciously adds, "Neither one can claim to have 'the whole truth.'"[46]

---

[43] Dietrich Bonhoeffer, *Life Together: The Classic Exploration of Christian Community* (New York: HarperOne, 1954), 53.
[44] Tyler and Grady, *Deceptive Diagnosis,* 21.
[45] Robert Schuller, *Self Esteem: The New Reformation* (Waco, TX: Word Books, 1982), 27.
[46] Schuller, *Self Esteem,* 27.

In his book, Schuller described exactly what this new reformation must entail:

> Where the sixteenth-century Reformation returned our focus to sacred Scriptures as the only infallible rule for faith and practice, the new reformation will return our focus to the sacred right of every person to self-esteem! The fact is, the church will never succeed until it satisfies the human being's hunger for self-value.[47]

This "sacred right" to self-esteem is the basis of the therapeutic model of preaching. In order to satisfy the human being's hunger for "self-value" Schuller is forced to reject the biblical description of man's inherent sinfulness. What is the core of Original sin according to Schuller? He answered, "Label it a 'negative self-image,' but do not say that the central core of the human soul is wickedness."[48] Schuller even goes so far as to assert, "For once a person believes he is an 'unworthy sinner,' it is doubtful if he can really honestly accept the saving grace God offers in Jesus Christ."[49] Ultimately, he is forced to radically redefine the whole notion of sin itself. Navigating far from the revelation of Scripture, Schuller wrote,

> What do I mean by sin? Answer: Any human condition or act that robs God of glory by stripping one of his children of their right to human dignity…I can offer still another answer: Sin is any act or thought that robs myself or another human being of his or her self-esteem.[50]

Of course, most preachers would not articulate these premises quite so boldly. They are much more subtle, but their preaching has become permeated with these noxious fumes. The biblical message stands in stark contrast to the psychological philosophies undergirding therapeutic preaching. About the same time psychology was making

---

[47] Ibid., 38
[48] Ibid., 67.
[49] Ibid., 98.
[50] Ibid., 14.

massive inroads to the church, Bonhoeffer poignantly described the inherent failures of secular psychology. He wrote,

> The greatest psychological insight, ability and experience cannot grasp this one thing: what sin is. Worldly wisdom knows what distress and weakness and failure are, but it does not know the godlessness of men. And so it also does not know that man is destroyed only by his sin and can be healed only by forgiveness.[51]

This conviction mirrors the biblical view of man, and if we are going to be faithful heralds of the divine message, it must be ours as well.

The Influence of the Seeker-Sensitive Movement

In more recent years the church has been enamored with the seeker-sensitive philosophy of ministry. At one time it seemed that virtually every denomination was swept up in its allure. If you have been in the church for any length of time, you have probably been affected by its influence, even if unwittingly. Under this model the church must become a place where the "unchurched" will feel comfortable and not threatened by the stereotypical church of yesteryear. Services incorporate contemporary music and even drama performed by professional quality performers—just under the level you might find at your local amusement park. These contemporary-styled services rapidly replaced the traditional Sunday worship and the birth of the mega-church was born. I do not know how many unchurched people these services ultimately drew, but I do know that a massive sheep transfer resulted as throngs left traditional churches in search of this innovative, fun, and entertaining phenomenon.

The Shrinking Sermon

This model had a massive impact not only upon the nature and understanding of preaching, but also upon the *length* of preaching. I know of no scientific research that has documented the evolving—or

---

[51] Bonhoeffer, *Life Together*, 119.

de-evolving—length of the sermon, but it is widely recognized that sermons are not nearly as long as they used to be. In the days of the Puritans, a sermon often lasted two hours or more. Today the average length of a conservative Protestant sermon is 21 to 30 minutes and a mainline Protestant church is 11 to 20 minutes.[52] Recently, the Vatican encouraged their priests to keep their homilies to eight minutes or less.[53] Obviously nothing in Scripture dictates the length of a sermon, and many people believe that the average attention span is drastically less than it used to be. While there may be some truth in that, I question the soundness of that reasoning. We can spend hours watching a movie or sporting event without blinking an eye. I am convinced that behind the shrinking sermon is the decreasing significance of the sermon's importance, not only in the role of worship, but all of life.

Felt-Needs

Beyond the length of the sermon, the seeker model has changed the nature of preaching itself. Undergirding the model is the philosophy that people will not respond to the biblical message if it is offensive and their personal needs are left unmet. Often the focus of the message is on the "felt needs" of people. Sermons are designed to help people live more fully and effectively in a hectic society. You are more prone to hear a sermon that stresses the practical over the doctrinal and the relational over the intellectual. These messages usually concentrate on people's pain, loneliness, and emotional hurts. Building better marriages and essentially satisfying the need for self-fulfillment are prominent topics.

When the ultimate goal is addressing "felt" needs, the significance and seriousness of sin is jettisoned for a watered down gospel offered at the altar of pragmatism, where the end justifies the means. Healing the

---

[52] Deborah Bruce, "Sermon Length," Beyond the Ordinary: Insights into U.S. Congregational Life, http://presbyterian.typepad.com/beyondordinary/2010/03/sermon-length.html (accessed 12/10/2011).

[53] Nick Squires, "The Vatican calls on priests to limit sermons to eight minutes," The Telegraph, http://www.telegraph.co.uk/news/religion/7429507/Vatican-calls-on-priests-to-limit-sermons-to-eight-minutes.html (accessed 12/10/2011).

"brokenness" of God's people (Jer 6:14) is reduced to market-savvy techniques that appeal and appease rather than a prophetic proclamation of spiritual transformation from death to life through a Spirit-empowered message that converts sinners. In Paul's ministry he was emphatic on this point: "My speech and my message were not in plausible words of wisdom, but in demonstration of the Spirit and of power, that your faith might not rest in the wisdom of men but in the power of God" (1 Cor 2:4–5).

In the seeker movement, secular philosophies of marketing and psychology have been wedded to the method and message of Christianity. The church growth movement has made an incredible impact upon the church in the last decades of the twentieth century. Rick Warren, one of the leading architects of the seeker sensitive movement, wrote the book, *The Purpose Driven Life,* which sold well over thirty million copies. That is a spectacular number even by secular standards. Many church leaders have been vigorously trained in this model, and it has been claimed that over four hundred thousand pastors and leaders have attended these church growth seminars. It is estimated that at one time nearly forty thousand church pastors and their congregations have patterned their churches after the seeker-friendly model. The impact has been incredible and has literally changed the face of the modern church in Western civilization. However, the new look bears little resemblance to the biblical Bride found in the New Testament.

The apostle Paul taught that preaching the Word is the hallmark of the church. In the world, the church is the "pillar and support of the truth" (1 Tim 3:15 NAS). He instructed Timothy, the young pastor, to preach the Word whether it was in style or not: Preach the Word in season and out (2 Tim 4:2). Moreover, for Paul, a significant element in preaching is to "reprove and rebuke" (2 Tim 4:2). When the church embraced the therapeutic model of preaching and its ultimate goal became a market-orientated approach to attract the "unchurched," one of the first causalities was the message about sin. The world has never taken kindly to the whole idea of sin, especially when you expose it or are against it.

A Two-edged Sword

True gospel preaching is a two-edged sword. It draws and disperses; it winnows the wheat from the chaff. It does offend; but it also offers the promise of healing and hope. As Peter Masters explains, "It not only convicts, persuades, woos, pleads, and warns with positive intent, but it also negatively offends and turns away impenitent, self-seeking or insincere people."[54] When the offense of the gospel is removed to draw in a crowd, it is fatally flawed. One can only imagine how one of these mega-churches would react to a Jonathan Edwards standing in their pulpit. It might take care of their parking problem. In its noble quest to attract the unchurched, the movement has unwittingly failed to bring people face to face with their ultimate problem: sin.

---

[54] Masters, *Physicians of the Souls*, 14.

> *Because of sin, humanity is under the curse and penalty of sin and bound for eternal judgment.*
>
> Page 46

Chapter Two - Culture and Sin

The Changing of the Guard at the Tomb of the Unknown Soldier is one of the great tourist attractions in Washington, D.C. At scheduled intervals throughout the day, people gather from all over the country to watch this momentous event. Soldiers that comprise the "Old Guard" come from a very elite class. For a person to apply for guard duty at the tomb he must be between 5' 10" and 6' 2" tall and his waist size cannot exceed 30". They must undergo rigorous training, including several hours a day of marching, rifle drill and uniform preparation. It is expected that there will be no wrinkles, folds or lint on their uniforms. The soldiers dress for duty in front of a full-length mirror, and it has been said that they may spend up to five hours a day getting their uniforms ready for guard duty. In light of the very public and ceremonial changing of the guard, I was amazed to learn that these soldiers guard that tomb twenty-four hours a day, seven days a week, through darkness, rain, sleet and snow. The public ceremonies are brief interruptions to the long hours of monotonous guard duty.

Culturally speaking, we are undergoing our own changing of the guard. Throughout the monotony of history there are periods of time when cultures experience massive transformations in the way that they think. The old views that dominated only a generation ago are (not always) quietly exchanged for a new way of thinking. We are living at such a time. As sociologists have examined various epochs of history they have observed that generations are often uniquely marked by distinct ways in which they view and interpret the world around them. These worldviews manifest themselves in literature, art, architecture, linguistics, and even religion.

Postmodernism and the Emergent Church

The name that has been given to the emerging culture is postmodernism, which as the name suggests, has itself emerged from modernity. While defining postmodernism has its challenges, numerous traits have formed some common denominators. Dan Kimball enunciated the contrasting traits postmodernism has to modernism. He described modernism as a "single, universal worldview and moral standard, a belief that all knowledge is good and certain, truth is absolute, individualism is valued, and thinking, learning, and beliefs should be determined systematically and logically."[55] In contrast, Kimball asserts that postmodernism holds that "all truth is not absolute, community is valued over individualism, and thinking, learning, and beliefs can be determined nonlinearly."[56]

Prevailing cultural worldviews have always presented challenges to the church. Gene Veith, Jr. wrote, "The church has always had to confront its culture and to exist in tension with the world. To ignore the culture is to risk irrelevance; to accept the culture uncritically is to risk syncretism and unfaithfulness."[57] Even though modernity was characterized by the fact that truth exists, a complementary trait to biblical Christianity, it nonetheless also poised serious challenges to biblical faith. Pastors who attempted to accommodate the Bible to modernity's scientific developments were often forced to compromise the biblical witness. For example, when evolution was elevated to a science rather than a theory, the supernatural account of creation in Genesis immediately became suspect. As modernism gave rise to the theory of theistic evolution, many scholars jettisoned the creation account for an allegorical interpretation.

However, over the years modernity ultimately failed to address many dimensions of life that science cannot answer, such as the soul or faith or the spiritual world. Somewhere in the mid-90s, sociologists observed the collapse of modernity and the rise of postmodernism. As noted, one of the hallmarks of postmodernity is the suspicion, if not outright rejection, of the concept of objective absolute truth. The suspicion of absolute truth has reverberated throughout the culture, most notably in the study of history, ethics, and religion. History itself is generally no longer viewed as fact, but rather someone's *perspective* of an event. Postmoderns generally understand apparent realities to be

---

[55] Dan Kimball, *The Emerging Church: Vintage Christianity for New Generations* (Grand Rapids: Zondervan Publishing, 2003), 49.
[56] Ibid., 49–50.
[57] Gene Veith, Jr., *Postmodern Times* (Wheaton: Crossway Books, 1994), xii.

nothing more than social constructs that are subject to change based upon one's perception or location. Thus, reality is relative and knowledge—or "knowability" about anything—is in doubt. One observer noted, "The hallmark of postmodern thought is the death of truth."[58] Truth is only a matter of one person's perspective, but each perspective is equally valid. Subsequently, in postmodernism tolerance becomes one of society's highest virtues. In fact the only thing a postmodernist cannot tolerate is intolerance.

While many evangelicals may be quick to dismiss the quagmire of postmodernity, we must recognize a number of valid concerns that postmodernity raises. The world is full of competing perspectives of reality. People are often blinded by their prejudices and one's perception of reality can be jaded. But this is not a new phenomenon. This has been a problem for thousands of years. With all his years in the machinery and treachery of Roman politics, one might almost sympathize with Pilate's dismissive question, "What is truth?" (John 18:38). For Christians, however, the problem of objective truth has been resolved: God's Word *is* truth (John 17:17). The only trustworthy perspective of reality is through the revelation of God through inspired human authors. Thus, the biblical worldview for the Christian is a deliverance from the quagmire of postmodernism. Christianity is built upon propositional truth, and in a world of uncertainty and competing perspectives, Jesus Christ announced that believers are set apart by the truth, which is the Word of God (John 17:17).

A New Kind of Christianity

Unfortunately, as many have observed, it seems that the church has been influenced more by the culture than influencing the culture itself. Postmodernity has spawned a whole new version of Christianity that has adapted the prevailing worldview of postmodernism into Christian thought. The religious offspring of postmodernism is the "emerging" church movement. It seems that rather than transforming the age with its message, the emerging Christianity is being transformed by the age. In this movement, propositional truth is highly suspect; truth, even

---

[58] Massimo Lorenzini, "Taking Every Thought Captive," http://www.frontlinemin.org/polemics.asp (accessed 8/14/2012).

God's truth, has become a matter of perspective not dogma. Such notions have had a chilling effect on the ministry of preaching.

Preaching Re-Imagined

In his book *Preaching Re-Imagined,* Doug Pagitt asserted that, "Preaching doesn't work,"[59] and "that preaching, as we know it, is a tragically broken endeavor."[60] Pagitt, who derisively calls the traditional delivery of a prepared message from a text "speaching,"[61] believes the church would profit more from a "progressional dialogue"[62] form of communication. According to Pagitt, progressional dialogue is a way to de-centralize the content of a message by incorporating the input of the congregation. In that way, the content of the sermon's message is no longer predetermined by a studied exegete, but rather develops as the audience adds their point of view.

According to Pagitt, progressional dialogue has a dangerous quality about it. He asks,

> What kind of faith will we have if the preselected, educated ones are not setting the agenda? What kind of faith will we have if our content is not prescreened and 'genericized' to meet the masses? What kind of faith will we have if regular people are putting their spin on it? What kind of faith will we have if we ask what the story has in mind for us? What kind of faith will we have if we listen to the outsider *and* the insider? What kind of faith will we have? Maybe a dangerous faith. Maybe a Christian faith. Maybe a faith worth preaching."[63]

Behind Pagitt's progressional dialogue is the prevailing worldview of postmodernism and his rejection of absolute truth. Acknowledging the

---

[59] Doug Pagitt, *Preaching Re-Imagined* (Grand Rapids: Zondervan Publishing, 2005), 18.
[60] Ibid., 19.
[61] Ibid., 18.
[62] Ibid., 23.
[63] Ibid., 46.

"uncertainty" and "fluidity" of the progressional dialogue upon the content of the sermon, Pagitt contends that truth is "progressive, not regressive or zero sum."[64] He asserts,

> Any conversation around the issue of truth benefits from a clarification of terms. When we talk about truth, we're really considering two concepts: reality (the way things are) and truth (a person's perspective of that reality). One of the problems with the use of the word *truth* is the adjectives people use with it: absolute, total, unquestioned, complete. These adjectives don't bolster truth; they redefine it. If what people mean when they use these qualifiers is that their view is the only view, then that isn't truth—at least by my definition. It's dogma, and it's rarely useful."[65]

A New Faith

It is beyond the scope of this work to enter into a long polemic against the emerging church. Ultimately, this movement will only flourish as long as postmodernism is the prevailing worldview. What happens post-postmodernism is anybody's guess, but for the time being this movement may be one of the most significant influences confronting the church. I am interested in the emergent movement for two reasons. First, the leaders of the emerging church are brazen in their quest to remake the Christian faith. Brian McLaren, commonly perceived to be an elder statesman of the group, wrote the book *A New Kind of Christianity: Ten Questions That Are Transforming the Faith* in which he makes it very clear that he is on a quest to reinvent the Christian faith. McLaren states that he is on "a quest for new ways to believe and new ways to live and serve faithfully in the way of Jesus, a quest for a new kind of Christian faith."[66] A new house or new car or new computer is fine, but there is one new thing we should have absolutely no interest in—a new faith, Christian or otherwise. We should be very

---

[64] Pagitt, *Preaching Re-Imagined*, 137.
[65] Ibid.,136.
[66] Brian McLaren, *A New Kind of Christianity: Ten Questions That Are Transforming the Faith* (New York: HarperCollins Publishers, 2010), 18.

nervous about anybody who espouses to reinvent a new kind of Christian faith. Yet that is exactly what McLaren is doing.

In 2005 Rob Bell, another prominent figure in the emerging church, published a provocative book entitled *Velvet Elvis*. If you are not familiar with the book, you might wonder how Elvis has anything to do with Christianity. Fortunately for us Bell explains the connection. Bell had in his basement a velvet painting of Elvis Presley from his glory days. He described the painting as a real work of art. But here is Bell's point: It is only *a* painting, one artist's rendition of the king of Rock-n-roll; it is not the ultimate or final rendition. There are many paintings of Elvis and probably many more to be made. For Bell, however, that painting of Elvis is a metaphor of Christianity and a signpost of his postmodern worldview. As a belief system, according to Bell, Christianity is a work of art in constant need of transformation and innovation. The full title of his book says it all: *Velvet Elvis, Repainting the Christian Faith.* Bell believes that a new perspective on Christianity is needed today, and in his own words, he is not talking about superficial changes. He wrote,

> By this I do not mean cosmetic, superficial changes like better lights and music, sharper graphics, and new methods with easy-to-follow steps. I mean theology: the beliefs about God, Jesus, the Bible, salvation, the future. We must keep reforming the way the Christian faith is defined, lived, and unexplained.[67]

I am a big believer in reformation because the church is always in need of reformation. *Ecclesia semper reformanda est* (Latin for "the church must always be reforming") was one of the basic tenets of the Protestant Reformation. The creeds and traditions of the church need constant and continual reevaluation according to the standard of Scripture, but these emerging church leaders have subtly misrepresented the notion of reformation. The Protestant Reformation was not about updating the Church or repainting it for a new generation—it was about taking the Church back to the truth of

---

[67] Rob Bell, *Velvet Elvis: Repainting the Christian Faith* (Grand Rapids: Zondervan Publishing, 2005), 12.

Scripture. *Sola Scriptura* was their cry. McLaren and company are not seeking reformation to the truth but alteration of the truth. They offer radical *re*definitions of basic Christian tenets.

For instance, McLaren urges us to "suspend what, if anything, you 'know' about what it means to call Jesus 'Savior' and to give the matter of salvation some fresh attention."[68] How does McLaren understand salvation? He writes,

> Let's start simply. In the Bible, *save* means "rescue" or "heal." It emphatically does *not* automatically mean "save from hell" or "give eternal life after death," as many preachers seem to imply in sermon after sermon. Rather its meaning varies from passage to passage, but in general, in any context, *save* means "get out of trouble." The trouble could be sickness, war, political intrigue, oppression, poverty, imprisonment, or any kind of danger or evil.[69]

It seems that sin has become so marginalized in McLaren's mind that rescue from sin's punishment fails to even be mentioned in his definition. However, the biblical understanding of salvation is quite clear. As Masters wrote, "The incontestable truth is that the term 'gospel' in Scripture is a most technical term that *always* refers to the persuasive presentation of soul-saving doctrines to lost sinners."[70]

A New Mission

This brings me to the second reason I am interested in the emergent movement. In the quest to remake or repaint Christianity, the mission of the church is being radically altered. Admittedly, many from within the emerging movement have been on the front lines of reaching out to the suffering and the hurting. They emphasize the need to alleviate poverty and racism and social injustice. They have been actively involved in noble undertakings like building orphanages and digging

---

[68] Brian McLaren, *A Generous Orthodoxy* (Grand Rapids: Zondervan Publishing, 2004), 101.
[69] Ibid.
[70] Masters, Physicians of Souls, 13.

wells for clean water in third world countries. They have also stressed the very popular notion of environmental stewardship. On the surface this all seems very noble and very Christian, but the underlying premises of these activities reveal startling theological aberrations.

The emerging movement is presenting a serious challenge to the focus that historic Christianity has placed upon sin, salvation, and eternity. Because of sin, humanity is under the curse and penalty of sin and bound for eternal judgment. Biblical Christianity is *other-world* orientated. The apostles commanded Christians to set their minds on things that are above, not on things that are on earth (Col 3:2). They reminded us that this world is not only temporary and passing away (1 John 2:17), but that we are strangers and aliens in this world, looking and waiting for a different homeland, that is, a heavenly one that has foundations whose designer and builder is God (Heb 11:10, 14–16).

Moreover, biblical Christianity has always been preeminently concerned with the eternal destinies that await all mankind. Heaven is the cherished hope of the believer; it is our true citizenship (Phil 3:20). The glory of heaven and being with Christ was so compelling to the apostle Paul that he could declare "to die is gain" (Phil 1:21). Furthermore, because humanity lives under the penalty of sin, the burden of the gospel has been carried to the nations because without Christ humanity is consigned to the eternal torments of hell. Throughout church history, the gospel has often been spread literally at the expense of the blood of the messenger.

All of this is being subtly challenged in the emerging movement. We are told that we need to quit focusing so much on the next life and start concentrating on changing *this* world. For example, Bell makes the audacious claim that, "For Jesus, the question wasn't how do I get to heaven? But how do I bring heaven here?"[71] What is revealed in the seemingly noble attempts to alleviate poverty and suffering in the world is a subtle form of universalism. In essence, the church needs to

---

[71] Bell, *Velvet Elvis*, 147.

quit worrying about saving souls and start helping the suffering and oppressed because ultimately everyone is going to heaven anyway.

The emerging movement asserts that Western Christianity has been overly preoccupied with the question of who is going to heaven or hell after death, and not focused enough on the question of what kind of life is truly pleasing to God here in the here and now. In an interview on the website Beliefnet, McLaren asserts,

> For many Christians, their faith is primarily about what happens to people after they die. That distracts them from seeking justice and living in a compassionate way while we're still alive in this life. We need to go back and take another look at Jesus' teachings about hell. For so many people, the conventional teaching about hell makes God seem vicious. That's not something we should let stand.[72]

Bell has been even more brazen in his redefining the orthodox concepts of hell. He wrote, "When people use the word hell, what do they mean? They mean a place, an event, a situation absent of how God desires things to be. Famine, debt, oppression, loneliness, despair, death, slaughter—they are all hell on earth."[73]

This radical reorientation of the Christian faith is having profound implications in the church. The historical method and message of reconciliation is being radically reimagined. Sin and its devastating effects upon humanity have been marginalized to a mere footnote. The emerging church sees the core problem of humanity as suffering, not sin. But the biblical witness is quite clear on this matter. Jesus Christ did not come to make the world a better place to live; He did not come to bring heaven here; He came to save sinners (Matt 1:21; Luke 19:10). Biblical Christianity is other-world orientated because the promise of the gospel is life in the age to come.

Recovering the Problem of Sin

---

[72] Brian McLaren, "Beyond Business-as-Usual Christianity," http://www.beliefnet.com/Faiths/Christianity/2005/05/Beyond-Business-As-Usual-Christianity.aspx (accessed 8/8/11).
[73] Bell, *Velvet Elvis*, 148.

These are just some of the forces that have succeeded in eradicating sin from our vocabulary. Yet, as followers of Christ and preachers of the gospel, we must come face to face with the message of the Bible. Over the next few chapters we will discover the problem of sin and its devastating effects upon humanity. From the beginning to the end, the focus of the Bible is upon *sin*. It opens with sin's entrance into the world and it ends with sin's judgment. There has never been a day when preaching about sin and the devastating effects of sin have been more important. Most people do not have a clue about the true nature of sin nor the wretchedness of their own. The one great problem of humanity is not poverty or disease or pollution or lack of self-esteem. The one massive problem of humanity is sin. Every societal disorder, every twisted, dysfunctional relationship, every broken marriage, every corrupt political regime, every earthly malady is the result of sin.

If we truly want to understand people and how they think and act, we must understand the problem of sin. If we move away from the reality and problem of sin, and make the Bible a handbook for successful living or just one perspective on life among others, the Bible not only becomes increasingly irrelevant, but preaching becomes archaic and the gospel a trifle. If alleviating suffering is the primary goal, the importance of the gospel proclamation is marginalized to a mere addendum. Today more than ever it is the preacher's role to explain the ultimate problem of sin and to expound upon the nature and devastating consequences of sin.

We have witnessed the denigration of the pastoral office to something like a life coach rather than an expert caretaker of the soul. We cannot expect the world to give the treatment of sinners back to the church; pastors must rise to the challenge. Understanding the anatomy of sin and treating it will require a boldness that has become increasingly uncommon in the pulpit today. Only to the degree that we understand the massive dimensions of sin will we be able to understand the incredible dimensions of salvation and grace.

The Impersonal Element of Preaching

It is my desire to recapture the unique role that preaching has in addressing the problem of sin. Masters wrote that preaching is "the most impersonal and yet the most personal exercise conceivable."[74] In essence, this is the genius of preaching. As an impersonal exercise, preaching lessens some of the stigma of confronting sin. Outside of a very intimate relationship with someone, confrontation is rare and often ugly. Unfortunately, our generation is inherently isolated from meaningful relationships. We crave privacy. In the old days, people built big front porches that often served as communal gatherings. Today, the most prominent feature of most homes is the garage. We prefer big decks in the backyard with privacy fences to preserve a shred of solitude in an ever-encroaching world. When it comes to sin, we are especially private. We prefer to keep our dirty laundry in the closet, and we do not take kindly when someone opens the door.

If you have ever been in a position of confrontation you know how difficult it can be. As a pastor I have been involved in these kinds of situations numerous times, and they are never pleasant. The cost of confrontation is considerably high. During the pre-confrontation, you can literally spend days and nights in agony awaiting the moment. You want to pray, "If possible let this cup pass from me..." The confrontation itself is uncomfortable and sometimes downright perilous. You might just be bringing a match to a fuse that is just waiting to be lit. There can be an explosion and you almost always get burned. People can get mad and offended. Tempers can flare. Only one word comes to mind: ugly.

If it is not enough that you spent countless hours agonizing over something you did not want to do in the first place, nor that the whole thing went badly, then you have to deal with the post-confrontation turmoil of reliving the whole thing, second guessing yourself, and being second guessed by others. Sadly, when you personally address the issue of sin with someone, you will often be criticized for *what* you said, *how* you said it, *when* you said it, and *why* you said it. "Monday morning quarterbacks" are a dime a dozen when it comes to something like this.

---

[74] Masters, *Physicians of the Soul*, 34.

Even though confronting sin will almost certainly be an unpleasant task, the Word of God expressly directs us here. Jesus was very explicit about the path that we are to follow as His disciples:

> Matthew 5:23-24—So if you are offering your gift at the altar and there remember that your brother has something against you, leave your gift there before the altar and go. First be reconciled to your brother, and then come and offer your gift.
>
> Matthew 18:15—If your brother sins against you, go and tell him his fault, between you and him alone.
>
> Luke 17:3—Pay attention to yourselves! If your brother sins, rebuke him, and if he repents, forgive him,

Confronting sin is clearly a personal responsibility of Christian discipleship, but it is very interesting to note the special charge that the New Testament epistles give to the overseers and pastors of the flock. In the course of ministry, especially it seems in the corporate ministry of the Word, the pastor is given the charge to "reprove" or "rebuke":

> 2 Timothy 4:2—Preach the word; be ready in season and out of season; *reprove, rebuke,* and exhort, with complete patience and teaching.
>
> Titus 1:13—This testimony is true. Therefore *rebuke them sharply*, that they may be sound in the faith.
>
> Titus 2:15—Declare these things; exhort and *rebuke with all authority*. Let no one disregard you.

The Scriptures plainly indicate that a preacher, in the course of preaching, is going to confront sin. It may be that within the corporate framework of this confrontation, the impersonal exercise is uniquely effective as a means of exposing individual sin from within the congregation. In essence, the preacher has a unique opportunity to address the individual problems of sin through the "mass mail" of a sermon. As Masters wonderfully explains, preaching has

> [R]emarkable advantages over personal conversations (and even the written word) because it combines an *impersonal* element with an intensely *personal* one. The preacher can say things that few would dare utter in personal witness…because preaching can touch the raw nerve, expose the ugliest sin, and lay bare the most impure motives of the heart. Yet at the same time it can appeal with very great concern and longing. It can achieve all this because the potentially offensive, invasive message is preached to a crowd, avoiding the possibility of insult and injury to individual listeners.[75]

Perhaps in the foolishness of preaching, the wisdom of God is again magnificently displayed. The preacher can say things corporately that could not be said privately without creating significant offense or a serious breach in personal protocol. The impersonal element of preaching affords the biblical message tremendous advantages. If offense is taken, it is not a personal offense; it is a Holy Spirit offense.

The Personal Element in Preaching

As Masters explains, preaching is "the most impersonal and yet the most personal exercise conceivable."[76] Under the ministry of preaching, the Holy Spirit has the power to make the indiscriminate message marvelously personal. This spiritual dynamic is the true genius of preaching. Spirit-empowered preaching presumes not only a Spirit-prepared message, but a Spirit-prepared people. It is humanly impossible for a preacher to craft a message uniquely tailored to each individual within the congregation. First, such a sermon would require an omniscient knowledge of each person's true spiritual condition, which is impossible. Secondly, it has been my experience that when I tried to tailor a sermon for someone I had in mind, that person was invariably not present that particular Sunday. After a few years of preaching to people who never come, you learn to spend your time preparing differently.

---

[75] Masters, *Physicians of the Soul*, 34–5.
[76] Ibid., 34.

As preachers, we need to be constantly reminded that the genius of preaching is not found in the ingenuity of the preacher but in the power of the Spirit. It is the Spirit who personalizes the truth of Scripture. When the truth is proclaimed in the dynamic of the Spirit, it should be common for many people to *think* that the message is aimed directly at them, even though the preacher is personally oblivious to their situation. That is why, in Masters' words, preaching is the "most impersonal and yet the most personal exercise conceivable."[77] In the following pages we will examine how preaching is perfectly suited for exposing the true nature of sin and the devastating effects it has upon our whole being.

---

[77] Masters, *Physicians of the Soul*, 35.

> *The chief end of the gospel is comfort, but it can only be offered to the disturbed.*
> Page 69

Chapter Three - The Sinfulness of Sin

Imagine that you are walking down the sidewalk on a lovely spring day, when you notice a car racing down the street. To your surprise it screeches to a halt right beside you. The driver rolls down the window and throws out a life preserver saying, "Please take this! It will keep you from drowning!" And with that he is gone. Most of us would think we were either a victim of a very bad practical joke or a witness of a lunatic. It is foolish to try to rescue someone who is not in trouble. Ironically, this is largely the situation that the church faces in the Western hemisphere. We are broadcasting the gospel to one of the most prosperous, pampered generations in all of history, and we herald the answer to a problem most people do not even realize they have. Today, the message of the gospel goes out to those who think that they are basically good people. Jesus made it clear, however, that His gospel will only be offered to the sinful.[78] Trying to give the gospel to people who fail to realize they are drowning in their sin is like throwing a life preserver to someone standing on a sidewalk.

Many pastors and evangelists would agree that it has become increasingly rare to find individuals burdened by sin. A person reeling under the weight of their sin is actually a precious find today. A number of years ago one of the elders of our church was involved in a training class for evangelism. They spent considerable time memorizing Bible verses pertinent to the gospel, and they learned to utilize a survey with a series of questions to steer conversations towards spiritual matters. After hours of preparation they would go out on the streets and put the program to work.

Ready to share the gospel, our elder and his team hit the streets of Los Angeles. Most of the encounters were cordial but fruitless. On one particular occasion, however, he and another trainee began a conversation with a young Hispanic woman. The trainee began with

---

[78] Matt 9:13; Mark 2:17; Luke 5:32.

the first survey question, "If you were to die today, what would you say if God asked you, 'Why should I let you into heaven?'" Surprisingly the young woman responded, "I wouldn't go to heaven. I would go to hell." The young trainee was obviously not ready for such a response. Others had dodged and hedged on that question countless times before; but not this time. Unprepared for her response, the trainee simply continued with the arranged questions on the survey. Finally our elder interrupted, "Did you hear her? She understands that she is not going to heaven." They put the survey away and this young woman was led to put her faith in Christ.

The Loss of Conviction

Although this was a wonderful story, it is also very rare. Most people do not overtly carry about a sentence of condemnation upon their hearts like this young woman did. The concept of sin has largely vanished from our vocabulary, but that does not mean that people do not believe in it. I am sure that many would still affirm its reality, at least to some extent. Most people will acknowledge that they have sinned, but the problem is that very few seem to recognize the *extent* of their sin. What is largely missing in this generation is what the Puritans labeled "the sinfulness of sin." Without the sinfulness of sin, the gospel is like throwing a life preserver to someone standing in a puddle. There is among us a dreadful ignorance and minimization of the evil of sin and its spiritual, emotional, physical, and psychological effects upon us. It should not be surprising that the minimization of sin is found in the culture at large because it is found in the church as well. Masters asserted that the "shallow treatment of sin is the most common fault of modern evangelicalism."[79] This shallow treatment of sin that is so common today is literally changing the story—the very plot and drama—of the Christian faith.

The drama of salvation is the grace of God bestowed upon undeserving sinners. Thus, sin is central to the story of Christianity. One of the most formidable literary works of the Christian faith in the Western hemisphere is John Bunyan's 17th century *Pilgrim's Progress*.

---

[79] Masters, *Physician of the Soul*, 63.

Bunyan is regarded not only as one of the most influential writers in human history, but he is, in fact, according to WorldNetDaily, the best-selling human author of all time.[80] *Pilgrim's Progress* has sold more copies than any other book in the world except for the Bible. This book has literally shaped the understanding of the Christian faith for generations. Charles Spurgeon claimed to have read it over a hundred times, and you will find hundreds of references to it throughout his preaching career.

I am convinced that this book has resonated over the centuries because Bunyan was able to brilliantly capture the drama of redemption experienced by millions of pilgrims down through the ages. We see our personal story in his allegory. I also believe that it has had such a lasting impact because page after page is permeated with Scripture. *Pilgrim's Progress* is one of the reasons Spurgeon once said of Bunyan, "Prick him anywhere; and you will find that his blood is Bibline, the very essence of the Bible flows from him. He cannot speak without quoting a text, for his soul is full of the Word of God."[81] *Pilgrim's Progress* is composed in the language of Scripture.

Sadly, this generation is largely unacquainted with this masterpiece. Bunyan's allegory opens with this simple line, "I saw a Man cloathed [*sic*] with rags, standing in a certain place, with his face from his own house, a Book in his hand, and a great Burden upon his back."[82] This great burden is central to the story and the catalyst that ultimately propelled Christian (Bunyan's main character) on a search for deliverance. On his journey he met a man named Evangelist who pointed him to the cross. Once he found the cross his heavy burden rolled into the empty sepulcher.

Although rare today, there have been periods in American history when the heavy burden of sin was much more prevalent than it is today. Those unique moments in our history have been called

---

[80] WND, "Discover the book that ranks 2nd only to the Bible," http://www.wnd.com/?pageId=38877#ixzz1hrOB4kfv (accessed 9/7/2011).

[81] Charles Spurgeon, *C.H. Spurgeon's Autobiography: His Diary, Letters, and Records* Vol. IV (1900; repr. Pasadena, TX: Pilgrim Publications, 1992), 268.

[82] John Bunyan, *The Pilgrim's Progress* (repr. Uhrichsville, OH: Barbour and Company, n.d.), 1. I have retained the archaic spelling as found in the book.

"awakenings," as in the First Great Awakening (early 18th century) and the Second Great Awakening (early 19th century). During these periods of revival people were awakened to spiritual realities and one of the defining characteristics was a deep awareness of sin among the people. James Boice wrote, "The Great Awakening was characterized by deep conviction of sin."[83] Jonathan Edwards preached his famous sermon "Sinners in the Hands of an Angry God" during just such a time, and the effects were incredible. It was reported that audible groans and shrieks from the congregation could be heard "a quarter-mile away."[84] The tumult was so great that Edwards was forced to stop his sermon several times. When I think how exciting and extraordinary it is for one young lady on the streets of Los Angeles to recognize her sinfulness and need of a Savior, I can hardly imagine what a whole church packed with such people must have looked like.

I think it is important to examine why the burden of sin, as a general rule, is rarely seen today. The burdened sinner has become a virtual endangered species. What is it that makes sin a burden? I believe it is the sinfulness of sin, the internal recognition of its evil, which makes it not only heavy but personal. The sinfulness of sin results in guilt and condemnation, and a burdened sinner is a prerequisite of the gospel. I am sure that is what Jesus meant when He said, "For I came not to call the righteous, but sinners" (Matt 9:13). Of course Jesus knew that no one is righteous, for all have sinned (Rom 3:23). There are only people who *think* they are righteous; and those are the people who have no part in the gospel. Jesus came to save those who *know* that they are sinners. If you are a sinner, the gospel is really good news.

Why has the burden of sin all but disappeared today? I am convinced that prevailing wrong views of God and of sin have decimated the ranks of the sinful. These erroneous views have successfully created a people who think they are basically good; and when they do begin to experience the pangs of sin, they are quickly convinced otherwise. If

---

[83] James Montgomery Boice and Philip Graham Ryken, *The Doctrines of Grace: Rediscovering the Evangelical Gospel* (Wheaton: Crossway Books, 2002), 52.
[84] George M. Mardsen, *A Short Life of Jonathan Edwards* (Grand Rapids: Eerdmans, 2008), 65–6.

we are going to recapture the sinfulness of sin, we must correct these prevailing attitudes.

Wrong Views of God

How we view our sin is generally a reflection on how we view God; and the right view of sin begins with the right view of God. When the great prophet of Israel saw the eternal God sitting on His throne, he heard heaven filled with the angelic refrain, "Holy, holy, holy is the LORD of hosts" (Isa 6:3). Holy means to be different, set apart. To repeat this attribute three times is not only unprecedented but almost inconceivable. God is infinitely different than we are, especially in moral purity. And when Isaiah realized this all he could say is "Woe is me…for I am a man of unclean lips" (Isa 6:5). We tend to think that if we get close to God we should get warm fuzzies; but in Scripture close encounters with God often resulted in intense psychological trauma. When God appeared, men had a nasty habit of falling on their faces.

The apostle Peter had a similar encounter with Christ on the lake of Gennesaret. After a night of fruitless fishing, Jesus instructed Peter to go back out and cast again his nets in the deep. Peter's response is classic. He said, "Master, we toiled all night and took nothing! But at your word I will let down the nets" (Luke 5:5). Scripture does not record what ran through Peter's mind before he said that, but it probably went something like this: "Jesus, You are a carpenter and, of course, a great teacher; but we are the professionals here. You should stick to teaching and leave the fishing to us." Nonetheless, Peter restrained himself and did what the Lord said, and they caught so many fish that even these professional fishermen were "astonished" (Luke 5:9).

I am not a very good fisherman (I drown more worms than catch fish), but I do know that catching fish can cause a lot of excitement. When Peter and his friends caught all those fish there was more than the thrill of the catch. These men were fishermen by vocation, and a catch which almost sank two boats represented a financial windfall. They probably made more money that day than they ever had before; but there was no backslapping or excited adrenaline in Peter's response. Peter saw a side of Jesus he had never seen before. Instead of a rebuke for his lack of faith, Peter saw in those fish a display of power and kindness from Jesus that he had never experienced and did not deserve. In that encounter with Christ's glory all Peter could say was, "Depart from me, for I am a sinful man, O Lord" (Luke 5:8). When you begin to see God for who He is, you start to see yourself for who you are.

Since our view of God is so instrumental in our understanding of sin, it is not surprising that the sinfulness of sin is such a rarity today. Although a lot of people believe in God, the problem is the *kind* of God in which they believe. Post-Christian America is biblically illiterate and lacking a biblical framework. Its apprehensions of God are woefully inadequate. I believe that we can see three major mistakes that abound in our culture.

Mistaking God for Man

God is holy, holy, holy—absolutely and utterly different and distinct from us. His thoughts and ways are not like ours; they are infinitely higher (Isa 55:8–9). Herein lies our problem: Apart from divine revelation, man cannot understand or know God. It is impossible for man to conceive of a Being beyond the constraints of our human intellect and experience. If you have ever traveled the world and seen blatant idolatry, you will notice how those idols always have human or earthly characteristics. Manmade gods will always have these characteristics because man cannot conceive of anything different. The apostle Paul understood this well. He wrote that men have "exchanged the glory of the immortal God for images resembling mortal man and birds and animals and reptiles" (Rom 1:23). It has been said that man was created in the image of God, and we have returned the favor by perpetually recreating God in our image.

Carved images of God are explicitly prohibited in the Ten Commandments (Exod 20:4). Material representations of God, which are limited to human contrivances, infinitely fail to adequately express His glory. If we look down through the corridor of time, man has built some pretty incredible things, but the best of them—the most glorious of them—would be blasphemously offensive to our Creator if they were meant to represent Him. The truth is that the biblically uninformed mental images of God today are equally blasphemous. If this is true, then the god that many of the 92% Americans say they believe in does not exist.[85]

Mistaking Mercy for Tolerance

A god created in the image of man will always carry inferior human characteristics. If you want to see just how debased they can be, read Greek mythology. The one thing a manmade god will not do is take sin seriously. As a fallen race, our desensitized notions of sin are propelled on to whatever divine being we create. Since we do not take sin seriously, we cannot imagine that He would either. Our natural ideas of God, yes, even Jehovah God, will always minimize His hatred of sin. In Psalm 50:16–21, God's charge against the wicked was their proclivity to assume that He was like them. It reads,

> But to the wicked God says: "What right have you to recite my statutes or take my covenant on your lips? For you hate discipline, and you cast my words behind you. If you see a thief, you are pleased with him, and you keep company with adulterers. You give your mouth free rein for evil, and your tongue frames deceit. You sit and speak against your brother; you slander your own mother's son. These things you have done, and I have been silent; *you thought that I was one like yourself*. But now I rebuke you and lay the charge before you. [emphasis added]

Notice carefully that it was God's silence about their sin that caused them to assume He was like them.

God has revealed Himself as a God of great mercy. He made Himself known to Moses proclaiming, "The LORD, the LORD, a God merciful and gracious, slow to anger, and abounding in steadfast love and faithfulness" (Exod 34:6). These incredible declarations about God are reiterated again and again throughout Scripture.[86] When His mercy is

---

[85] This statistic was taken from a Gallup poll in 2011. Frank Newport, "More Than 9 in 10 Americans Continue to Believe in God," (accessed 12/5/2011) http://www.gallup.com/poll/147887/americans-continue-believe-god.aspx

[86] Ps 31:19; 86:5, 15; 103:8–13; 111:4; 112:4; 116:5; 145:8; Joel 2:13; Mic 7:18; Rom 2:4; Eph 1:7–8.

measured it is as high as the heavens (Ps 36:5; 57:10). He is longsuffering toward the sinner, restraining His holy wrath and justice (Num 14:18; Jonah 4:2; Nah 1:3). His abounding love causes Him to be ready to forgive all who turn to Him (Neh 9:17). These precious attributes that grace our world every day are the only reasons that keep any rebel to His law from being immediately consumed.

Man, however, misconstrues the mercy of God. He makes the fatal assumption that God's silence means that He is apathetic toward man's sin (Ps 50:21–22), and this propels men further into sin. H.C. Leupold wrote,

> Such an idea may grow out of the practical observation made by many that iniquity is not always punished at once. It is seemingly not punished at all if by punishment one means swift and immediate punishment. God's mill grinds slowly. The wicked fail to see that fact. So the poor wicked man labors under the delusion that there is not retribution: that he can get away with what he does, and shapes his course accordingly.[87]

As Solomon observed, "Because the sentence against an evil deed is not executed speedily, the heart of the children of men is fully set to do evil" (Eccl 8:11). Burroughs wrote, "Because there is no attribute abused to be an abettor to sin more than is the mercy of God. It is abused and made to harden the hearts of men and women in sin. There is no attribute so abused."[88] Tolerance is, perhaps, the premiere virtue of our day. The only thing tolerant people cannot tolerate is intolerance. Tolerance does not judge another person; and because God does not immediately judge sin, the world believes that God is also tolerant. Man inherently mistakes mercy for tolerance, but this innate misconception is a fatal error. According to Paul, God's mercy is intended to lead to repentance not apathy (Rom 2:4–6).

---

[87] H.C. Leupold, *Exposition of the Psalms* (Grand Rapids: Baker Books, 1969), 294.
[88] Burroughs, The Evil of Evils, 53.

Mistaking Love for Sentimentality

I believe that one of the most significant factors in the minimization of sin's sinfulness is the emphasis that is placed upon the love of God today. If there is one thing that the 92% of Americans who believe *in* God believe *about* God it would be that He is loving. Of course, love is without question a pre-eminent attribute of God; but in his book, *The Love of God,* John MacArthur begins the first sentence of his book with this sobering assessment, "Love is the best known but least understood of all God's attributes."[89] The emphasis that God's love has received today has come at the cost of His other attributes; and love divorced from holiness and absolute power and infinite wisdom is a love of men not God.

If we could paint the image that many seem to have of God today, we might end up with a portrait of a kindhearted grandfather who waits in heaven to help when needed. It may be hard for us to believe in this day and age, but such an image would not have existed a generation or two ago. In fact, only a few hundred years ago, the most prominent image people had of God was not a kindhearted grandfather, but a watchmaker. During the 17th and 18th centuries Deism was a prominent form of belief in which God created the universe then stepped aside to let it run on its own—the way a watchmaker would with a watch. The idea of a personal God who intervened or even cared about the affairs here below would have been very foreign to their way of thinking.

What may be harder to believe is that in previous generations the love of God did not enjoy the prestige that it does today. When people thought about God, it was not love that came to their mind. I know it is hard to imagine someone actually thinking differently than we do, but they did. If we look to the Puritans and their theology of God, love was much less conspicuous than it is today. Several years ago I took our church through a study on the attributes of God. One of my main resources was the work of Stephen Charnock, *The Existence and Attributes of God.* It is recognized as one of the most thorough treatments on the nature of God in print. It is a massive two-volume set

---

[89] John MacArthur, *The Love of God* (Dallas: Word Publishing, 1996), 1.

containing over eleven hundred pages of material. Charnock covered, among other things, God's power, His wisdom, His goodness, and His dominion. However, out of all the material that he amassed on the attributes of God, you would search in vain for a chapter on the love of God. In fact, the subject index in the back of his book records only four pages in which the love of God appears. Out of eleven-hundred pages of material, Charnock covered the subject of the love of God in four disparate paragraphs.

I am not suggesting that Charnock was right to overlook the love of God; he was not. My purposes in highlighting a past generation's view of God is to demonstrate how influential a prevailing culture (even in the church) can be on one's understanding of God, whether it is biblical or not. It is amazing, if not downright scary, how much influence a culture can have on our beliefs. In former days, the justice and dominion and holiness of God were often stressed to the point that His love was almost forgotten. Our culture, however, has been influenced by a caricature of God that makes it incredibly difficult to understand or articulate the biblical concept of His love.

Today, the predominant view of the love of God is rooted more in folklore (the common beliefs of the culture) than biblical theology, and it looks a lot more like mushy sentimentalism than holy, sovereign love. In his book, *The Difficult Doctrine of the Love of God,* D.A. Carson wrote, "The love of God has been sanitized, democratized, and, above all sentimentalized."[90] Sentimentalism is a weak emotionalism that emphasizes sentiment over reason. This sappy love has spawned a new genre of Christian music that a number of people have characterized as "God-is-my-boyfriend-music." No wonder that many men do not want to have anything to do with church. This sentimental view of God's love fits the pattern of a manmade god whose wrath is not aroused by sin, but loves and accepts us just the way we are. Most people are assured of God's acceptance, even *without* the gospel.

---

[90] D.A. Carson, *The Difficult Doctrine of the Love of God* (Wheaton: Crossway Books, 2000), 11.

Because our view of God is so instrumental in our understanding of sin, these mistaken notions of God that prevail in our culture have had an incredibly chilling effect on the sinfulness of sin. It should not surprise us that we rarely see people burdened by sin. People are still burdened, certainly; but because we have lost a biblical framework, the burden is attributed more often to unexplained depression or poor self-esteem, rather than to the weight that a guilty sinner has before an offended God. Losing a biblical framework seriously jeopardizes the gospel, because these erroneous notions have ultimately skewed our view of sin.

The Wrong View of Sin

The god of American folklore that winks at sin and "loves us just the way we are" radically distorts our view of sin. Sin is often viewed as simple indiscretions or accidents. These weak apprehensions of sin can be seen in the anemic way that people apologize for their wrong behaviors. How many times have you heard someone say, "I am sorry; I didn't mean to…?" What does that mean? Ultimately, it is a feeble excuse that lessens the stigma of the perpetrator. It is the difference between accidently kicking someone and deliberately kicking them. A deliberate kick is much worse than an accidental one. Sin is so evil and vile precisely because it comes from the wicked intentions of the heart. Can you imagine an apology that said, "I am sorry; I am so vile and selfish and mean. Please forgive me?"

The Confession of Sin

Confession of sin is at the heart of Christianity, but what does confession mean? Those from a Roman Catholic background might envision the confessional box in which they disclose their wrongs to a priest. In evangelism people are often told that they must "admit that they are a sinner." In 1 John 1:9 the apostle said, "If we confess our sins, He is faithful and just to forgive our sins…" In Greek the word "confess" is a compound word (*homo-legeō*), and it is the combination of these two words that, I believe, really gets to the heart of what confession of sin means.[91] This compound word literally means "to say the same thing." Thus, when we confess our sins to God, we say the same thing about our sin that He does. This, then, is a monumental confession.

We have an example of just such a confession recorded for us in the Bible from David after he was confronted for his adultery and murder. David prayed,

> Have mercy on me, O God, according to your steadfast love; according to your abundant mercy blot out my transgressions. Wash me thoroughly from my iniquity, and cleanse me from my sin! For I know my transgressions, and my sin is ever before me. Against you, you only, have I sinned and done what is evil in your sight, so that you may be justified in your words and blameless in your judgment. Behold, I was brought forth in iniquity, and in sin did my mother conceive me (Ps 51:1–5).

There are several facets in this passage that are helpful in explaining the nature of confession. First, David acknowledged that his actions were "transgressions" against the Law of God. Transgression is a strong word describing an act of rebellion or revolt. This is not "I am sorry, I didn't mean to…" Rebellion is not an accident. The depth of this confession is compelling. David acknowledged the willful intentions of his heart. It is like saying, "This is so bad because I meant to do it." This becomes evident as David's confession goes even deeper.

Secondly, David asked to be washed from his "iniquity." According to Leupold, the Hebrew word for iniquity (*'awon*) connotes "perversion and twisting of moral standards."[92] This is recognition of something deeper than even rebellion. David confessed that deep within his soul he was crooked and bent toward evil. He said, in essence, "I rebelled because I have a crooked heart." In fact, David confessed that he was

---

[91] Determining a word's meaning solely from its root origin is common fallacy in word studies; however, in this case I believe the root words are instrumental in conveying at least one of the nuances (confess) and perhaps could even be instrumental in the others (promise, agree, declare, or praise).

[92] Leupold, *Exposition of the Psalms*, 401.

born with a crooked heart.[93] This explains what verse 5 means, "Behold, I was brought forth in iniquity, and in sin did my mother conceive me." He is not blaming his sin on his mother; rather he is acknowledging that he was inherently sinful even at birth. He is describing what theologians would later call Original sin. He had a twisted moral nature that was bent toward sin. David longed to have this perverse nature washed, which is why he prayed, "Create in me a clean heart" (Ps 51:10).

Thus, we have in David's confession a complete agreement with God about his sinfulness. Gerald Wilson wrote, "The psalmist's confession is far-reaching and complete."[94] God knew David's heart and David's confession agreed with God's verdict. The great burden that rested on David was the fact that his offense was against God. Sometimes we see people express remorse only when they experience the consequences of their sin; other times people experience sorrow when they see the hurt they have caused other people. In David's case, he had not yet experienced any consequences to his sin, so it was not the consequences that made him sorry. Additionally, David had to know that his actions had hurt many people. He caused tremendous damage. He tore apart a marriage; he murdered an innocent man; he robbed a mother of her son, and a wife of her husband. But even this did not cause David his greatest burden. He wrote, "Against you, you only, have I sinned and done what is evil in your sight" (Ps 51:4). The heart of David was broken because he had sinned against God. David understood the sinfulness of his sin. As Venning wrote, "The sinfulness of sin not only appears from, but consists in this, that it is contrary to God."[95]

The Preacher's Responsibility

As ministers of reconciliation, the preacher has a vital role in correcting the false apprehensions of God and sin that permeate our land. Like *Pilgrim's Progress,* we can only reclaim the knowledge of

---

[93] This is, in fact, the rendering of Ps 51:5 in several English translations: NET—"Look, I was guilty of sin from birth." NIV—"Surely I was sinful at birth." NRS—"Indeed, I was born guilty."
[94] Gerald Wilson, *The NIV Application Commentary,* Psalms Vol 1, (Grand Rapids: Zondervan, 2002), 774.
[95] Venning, *Sinfulness of Sin*, 29.

God and sin through the language of Scripture, but it will not come cheaply. During periods of revival in the Old Testament, the idols that littered the land were torn down and thrown away.[96] It is time for the preacher to tear down the manmade images of folklore and throw them away. Isaiah envisioned in the New Covenant messengers who would proclaim, "Your God reigns" (Isa 52:7). I am convinced that one of our greatest priorities is to recover the greatness of God in our preaching. We do not have time to trifle away precious minutes. We need to give our people a fresh vision of God's power and glory. In his book, *The Supremacy of God,* John Piper wrote,

> It is not the job of the Christian preacher to give people moral or psychological pep talks about how to get along in the world; someone else can do that. But most of our people have no one in the world to tell them, week in and week out, about the supreme beauty and majesty of God.[97]

I am struck by that phrase, "no one in the world to tell them." If the preacher does not stand up and reclaim God from the box of current conceived notions that have tamed Him, who will?

We really need to consider what it means to take God out of the box our world has made. Natural inclinations of God fit neatly in packages that can be understood and explained. The God of Israel is not such a God. We need to understand that biblical encounters with God invariably produce trauma. Even a godly man like Job, who thought he knew God, was humiliated by his inadequate comprehensions when he encountered Him. He confessed, "I heard of you by the hearing of the ear, but now my eye sees you; therefore, I despise myself, and repent in dust and ashes" (Job 42:6). Even Job had God in a box, but it was blown away.

If a preacher is going to be a faithful messenger, it should be expected that trauma and tension would be an integral part of his sermon. The holiness of God and His law will traumatize a sinner, and His wrath

---

[96] For example see Asa in 1 Kgs 15:12 and Manasseh in 2 Chr 33:15.
[97] John Piper, *The Supremacy of God in Preaching* (Grand Rapids: Baker Books, 1990), 12.

against sin will create a tension in His love towards the sinner. Yet this is almost anathema today. Stott wrote, "Every preacher needs to be both a Boanerges (having the courage to disturb) and a Barnabas (having the charity to console)."[98] The chief end of the gospel is comfort, but it can only be offered to the disturbed. Unfortunately, we have become so preoccupied with making people feel comfortable in church that we have jettisoned the trauma and tension necessary for the relief and release of the gospel. The result is that sin never becomes sinful, and the grace in the gospel never becomes amazing. The preacher who is able to retain the biblical tension between law and gospel will never have to worry about keeping people's attention.

---

[98] John Stott, *Between Two Worlds: The Art of Preaching in the Twentieth Century* (Grand Rapids: Eerdmans Publishing, 1982), 315.

One of the primary goals of preaching is not to make people feel better but to make them think rightly.
Page 78

Chapter Four - The Mind and Sin

Years ago I got tired of having a car payment, so I sold our car and bought an old beater. The gray dull paint had faded off most of the hood and none of the wheels had hubcaps. Probably the worst part of it all was that it was a station wagon. I take that back. The worst part was that the ignition switch did not work, and I literally had to use a crowbar to start the car; but none of that deterred me. I drove that car around everywhere with pride. Truthfully, it was a fairly good car with some unique features. For instance I never had to worry about locking my doors because nobody in their right mind would ever think of stealing it. I rarely wasted money on car washes, and I laughed at hailstorms. Over time, however, my money-saving endeavor did not work quite the way I planned. One morning the car would not start, so I towed it to a mechanic who diagnosed the problem as a malfunction in the engine's computer module. Frankly, I had no idea my car had anything resembling a computer in its design; nevertheless, I decided to replace the module and keep driving my dream machine. Incredibly, it happened again. After replacing the module for the *third* time I realized I was fighting a losing battle. Even though everything else worked fine, once that computer failed, it affected everything. So it is with us. Our mind controls everything we do, and once it is corrupted it affects everything we do.

The mind is an incredible machine. Every day it processes thousands of bits of information from which we interpret and respond to life around us. The process of analyzing all the information around us results in the formation of our ideas and perspectives. In our world, perspective is everything; in fact, perspective becomes our *reality*. The danger is that our perspectives can often be mistaken or flawed. Perhaps the largest optical illusion in the world is the St. Louis arch in my home state of Missouri. If you look at it with the naked eye, your mind processes the information and forms the idea or perception that the arch is much taller than it is wide; but it is not. It is exactly as tall as it is wide. *However, the things that we perceive to be true are often more compelling than what is actually true.* The truth is that our perceptions—right or wrong—profoundly influence how we think and respond to the world around us.

The Personification of Sin

When Watson wrote his book on the mischief of sin, he was referring to the evil or harm caused by sin. When we speak of sin causing evil or harm, it is clear that sin becomes something more than just what we do. Sin takes on a life of its own. According to the apostle Paul, once sin entered the world everything changed. More than any other author of Scripture, Paul expounded upon the nature of sin and its consequences upon humanity. It is fundamentally important for us to understand that sin *is a power at work within us*. Watson wrote, "If you consider what power sin has in a man, it is a miracle that he should forsake it. Sin is a man's self, like a member of the body which is not easily parted with. Sin is woven and incorporated into the nature of a man. It is as natural to sin as for fire to burn."[99] Douglas Moo wrote that in Romans the apostle Paul "personifies sin, picturing it as a 'power' that works actively and purposefully."[100] The personification of sin gives sin life-like characteristics that operate within our own personality.

In Romans 7 Paul described several aspects to the personality and power of sin as it operates in our life:

- Sin "seized" an opportunity (v. 8)
- Sin "produced" more sin, it multiplied itself (v. 8)
- Sin "came alive" (v. 9)
- Again, sin "seized" an opportunity (v. 11)
- Sin "deceived" him (v. 11)
- Sin "killed" him (v. 11)

Paul proceeds to describe this "person" of sin operating within us as literally creating schizophrenia in the human soul. Paul wrote, "I do not understand my own actions. For I do not do what I want, but I do the very thing that I hate…So now it is no longer I who do it, but sin

---

[99] Watson, *The Mischief of Sin*, 66.
[100] Douglas Moo, *The Epistle to the Romans,* The New International Commentary on the New Testament (Grand Rapids: Eerdmans Publishing, 1996), 436.

that dwells within me" (Rom 7:15,17). Sin hijacks a person by taking over the command and control center of their very being.

Like a cancer, sin becomes alive and grows within us. There is a progression in the power of sin, as one sin leads to another and a little sin becomes a greater sin. Sin is such a formidable foe because it takes on a life of its own within us and begins begetting and breeding more and more sin, so that it overpowers us. Under such dominion one cries out, "It is no longer I who do it, but sin that dwells within me!" (Rom 7:20). This personification of sin was not the invention of the apostle. Thousands of years earlier, the Lord warned Cain, "Sin is crouching at the door. Its desire is for you" (Gen 4:7). Cain should have been shocked to consider that just outside his "door" was this thing, this being, something lurking close by crouching like a lion. It was *sin*—and its desire was for him! Ironically, although we have much more revelation about sin than Cain, we manifest a similar lackadaisical attitude toward it.

The personification and power of sin should be shocking to us. Sin is nearby; its desire is for us, and once sin enters, its domination is assured. The power of sin at work within us is real. It makes us do evil things; it makes us do stupid things. The language Paul used almost two thousand years ago to describe the work of sin is not unfamiliar to us today at all. Every man can relate to what Paul wrote in Romans 7:15, "I do not understand my own actions. For I do not do what I want, but I do the very thing I hate." Have not you felt that within your own soul as well? We know the struggle. We feel the fight; but we have been conditioned to call it something else. We underestimate the spiritual power of sin. Today, we call the state of being under the dominion of sin an "addiction." We might be told that we have "psychological" issues, or maybe even a "chemical imbalance;" but nobody wants to believe that they are sinners under the power of sin. Addiction is nothing less than the power of sin at work within us, causing us to do the things that we do not want to do.

Distorted Perspectives

At one of the most fundamental levels of our existence, sin affects the mind. The corruption of the mind is the epicenter of all sin's mischief in our life. It distorts and twists our powers of perception in dramatic fashion. From the moment sin entered the world, its first target was the mind. Satan launched a full-scale attack on Eve's mind by distorting what she thought about God and His command. Being deceived, she took of the forbidden fruit, gave it to her husband and he ate. Significantly, the very first effect of sin recorded about Adam and Eve was that "the *eyes* of both were opened, and they knew that they were naked" (Gen 3:7) [emphasis added]. Of course, it was not their physical eye that was affected; it was their mind, the command and control center of their very being. They immediately began to perceive themselves and each other in a very different light.

In an excellent little essay entitled "What is Sin?" David Powlison remarked that we tend to think of sin only as consciously willed acts—things that we do; but sin is that and so much more. As Powlison explained, "Sin includes what we simply are, and the perverse ways we think, want, remember, and react. Most sin is invisible to the sinner because it is simply how the sinner perceives, wants, and interprets things."[101] This is one of the most subtle but profound ways that sin affects us. Sin creates in the mind a perverted filter that distorts our perception of life and people and even ourselves! It literally becomes the lens through which we view life. Once the command and control center of our being is corrupted, every component of our life is corrupted. The indelible effect of sin upon the mind is recorded all throughout Scripture. Paul said of fallen humanity, "they became futile in their *thinking* and their foolish hearts were darkened" (Rom 1:21) [emphasis added]. In Ephesians, Paul urged believers to conduct themselves differently than unbelievers who live life "in the futility of their *minds*...darkened in their understanding" (Eph 4:17-18) [emphasis added]. Peter O'Brien wrote that this mindset "was so

---

[101] David Powlison, "What is Sin?" *The Journal of Biblical Counseling* 25, No. 2 (Spring 2007), 25–6.

distorted that it was marked by *futility* and had fallen prey to folly"[102] [emphasis his].

Evil Imaginations

Engulfed in futility, the mind becomes a cesspool of sin. For example, God's assessment of the human race before the flood is staggering. Genesis 6:5 says, "The LORD saw that the wickedness of man was great in the earth, and that every intention of the thoughts of his heart was only evil continually." The Hebrew word for "intention" is *yetser* and it means to form or to fashion. It refers to human plans or intensions. The King James Version translates it more graphically with the word *imagination*—"every imagination of the thoughts of his heart was only evil continually." As God looked upon humanity, He saw that the imaginations, the mental constructs shaped by their thoughts, the musings of their mind, were continually evil. Under the influence of sin the mind becomes a cesspool of distortion, breeding and begetting all kinds of sinful thought-constructs. Sin manufactures mental structures within the mind from which we build hypothetical scenarios, make choices and judgments, and devise plans and carry out purposes. Though invisible to us, they are seen by God, and they are all corrupt. As Boston wrote, "The heart is ever framing something, but never one thing right."[103]

Sin is never static; it is incremental and progressive. Sin builds mental perspectives from which we view everything. The more we give in to sin and entertain it, the more it takes over our mind, and the more elaborate and distorted our mental constructs become. If you thought this was only a problem *before* the flood, you would be mistaken. After the flood, when God promised never to destroy the earth by a deluge of water again, He said, "I will never again curse the ground because of man, for the intention of man's heart is evil from his youth" (Gen 8:21). Man's mental constructs—all his "imaginations"—are corrupted, even from our youth.

---

[102] Peter O'Brien, *The Letter to the Ephesians,* The Pillar New Testament Commentary (Grand Rapids: Eerdmans Publishing, 1999), 320.

[103] Thomas Boston, *Human Nature in Its Fourfold State* http://www.reformationfiles.com/files/displaytext.php?file=boston_humannature.html (accessed 6/13/2011).

The Psalmist also described sin as an active, energetic force that infiltrates and influences the mind. He wrote, "Transgression speaks to the wicked deep in his heart..." (Ps 36:1). Sin starts talking to you and shaping your thoughts and desires; and as it talks to you it sounds strangely like yourself. From these thought constructs, the sinner "flatters himself" (Ps 36:2). What comes from his mouth are "trouble and deceit," (Ps 36:3) and he ceases "to act wisely and do good" (Ps 36:3). From these corrupt imaginations "he plots trouble while on his bed; he sets himself in a way that is not good; he does not reject evil" (Ps 36:4). The mind infected with sin is like a computer infected with a virus—it starts doing strange things.

Think with me for a moment how this works. Let bitterness into your mind and it starts talking to you. Bitterness begins to build elaborate mental constructs—vain imaginations that filter not only how you perceive life but how you interpret other's actions. Once bitterness towards someone takes root in the mind it doesn't matter what that person does; it will always be misconstrued. Once you become embittered toward a spouse or co-worker or neighbor, everything they do will be suspect. Such unchecked bitterness has split churches and destroyed marriages. The same goes for sins like jealousy. Let jealousy in and it starts talking to you. The mind begins to process elaborate constructs of mistrust and doubt. Every action, no matter how innocent it may be, is filtered through a distorted lens and the result is always destructive.

Who can deny the distortion of reality that unbridled lusts cause? Inordinate desires for anything, flesh or shiny metal, quickly catapult the mind out of the realm of reality into a world of make believe. We call such a world "fantasy," which the dictionary ironically defines as "a mental image, especially when unreal or fantastic." In a man, carnal lusts create a woman that really does not exist. Covetous desires build expectations that material possessions can never deliver. No doubt this is why the apostle calls the unregenerate mind "futile"— empty, worthless.[104]

---

[104]Rom 1:21; Eph 4:17

We can see the imaginations of sin at work when we let worry or fear take hold in our thoughts. Anxiety afflicts millions of Americans and it is one of the most prevalent problems found in the church. We do not tend to view anxiety or worry as sin, yet according to Scripture it is undoubtedly so. Anxiety is not of faith, and whatever is not of faith is sin (Rom 14:23). Anxiety carries with it all the active components of sin. Once it enters the mind it begins to concoct all manner of despairing scenarios that feed our fear and terrorize our mind. We have all heard that most of the things we worry about never materialize, but that does not stop our mind from constructing bulwarks of doom. Once the sin of worry enters the mind it begins to work on the imaginations of the heart.

Living Under a Delusion

Under the power of sin, our thoughts are no longer rooted in reality. We begin to view life and judge people under false delusions. In this beguiled state, we interpret people's actions through screwed up filters. Most people are absolutely clueless to the distorted constructs under which they live and interpret the life around them. After all, their mental constructs have become their own reality. Ecclesiastes 9:3 says, "The hearts of the children of man are full of evil, and *madness* is in their hearts while they live." The "madness" here carries the idea of being delusional. According to Solomon, while people live with evil in their hearts, they are literally living under a delusion. We stew over petty contrivances of offense and form false mental constructs by which we interpret life and other people's action and we judge them accordingly. In light of sin's distortion of the mind it is a miracle that we are able to have any meaningful relationships in our life. We build these false constructs in our mind through jealously, self-centeredness, bitterness, and fear, and then we extrapolate them on those around us.

One day while I was studying upstairs in my office, I received a text from my wife. She had gone to the store but accidentally left her grocery list on the kitchen table. In her text she asked me, "Would you be so kind to text me the grocery list. Left it on counter." Admittedly, it was a little frustrating, but being the wonderful husband that I am I decided to help her out. So I stopped everything that I was doing, went downstairs, and—not being the best texter in the world—laboriously typed out her grocery list for her. I went back upstairs and resumed my study. I noticed, however, after about ten minutes that my wife never responded to my text. Now I was more than a bit perturbed. The whole thing reeked of ingratitude to me.

As I stewed over the situation the conclusion was obvious: Here I was, engaged in the high and holy calling of studying God's Word, and I was rudely interrupted. I had been greatly inconvenienced to do something that really was not my responsibility. Obviously my wife did not respect the importance of my work or the seriousness of the inconvenience. I could not let such injustice go unrequited. Masking what I really wanted to say, I decided to send her another text which simply said, "U R WELCOME." Yes, I employed the power of all-caps. After about fifteen minutes I finally got this reply: "Honey so sorry. Phone was in purse. Never heard it. Please forgive me." Why she would ask me to text the grocery list to her, but not keep her phone handy is a subject I would have to address in a different book. We both laugh about it now, but honestly it is pretty pathetic. I had extrapolated on my wife an ingratitude and disrespect that never existed. Yet in my mind I acted upon them as a reality. This particular incident might be considered comical, but I could probably find scores of other episodes in my life that are not nearly so funny. Sin always makes us delusional. This story illustrates how quickly and easily the mind succumbs to false mental constructs from which we interpret life and judge people. As Pawlison remarked, "Most sin is invisible to the sinner because it is simply how the sinner perceives, wants, and interprets things."[105]

Preaching to the Mind

Recognizing these corrupted mental structures informs us that preaching must primarily be directed towards the *mind*. The manifestation of truth through the proclamation of the Word requires a change in thinking. One of the primary goals of preaching is not to make people feel better but to make them think rightly. One of the most significant aspects of preaching towards the mind is found within the word *remind,* or re-mind, to cause to remember, to bring to the

---

[105] Powlison, "What is Sin?", 26.

mind again. The apostle Peter described his own ministry in terms of stirring up believers "by way of *reminder*" (2 Pet 1:13) [emphasis added]. Preaching is not finding novelties or following the most recent fad. It is not just an appeal to emotions; manipulating emotions is easy. For many people, preaching will be the passionate reiteration of truth that is *already known*.

Unfortunately, in our "Christian-ese" important words, heavy words, powerful words, become light and airy and virtually meaningless. Familiarity breeds meaninglessness. Many important biblical words have become cliché, being casually thrown around—usually right over our heads. Consider for a moment the number of exhortations in Scripture that specifically address the mind. For example, important words like *repentance* or *repent*, *remember*, *consider*, or *reckon*. We find these words all throughout our English Bibles, but they have become trivial. Sadly, our eyes can gloss over these words as quickly as they do when we scan through junk mail. We need to hear these words afresh.

Although we do not hear much about repentance anymore, when we do use this word most people only have vague, esoteric concepts of what it means. Repentance (*metanoia*) literally means to change the mind. John the Baptist came preaching, "*Repent* for the kingdom of God is at hand" (Matt 3:2) [emphasis added]. John's message was, "change your mind" because the kingdom of God was near. He called upon people to change the way they were thinking about things. Changing the way you think changes the way you behave. Preaching that focuses on behaviors rather than corrupted, sinful thinking processes, promotes either moralism or legalism but not genuine righteousness.

Another similar word we fail to grasp the importance of is *remember*. It was a word God used again and again in instructing Israel. The Lord actually told Israel to put tassels on their garments to constantly remind them of His commandments. Numbers 15:37–40 says,

> The LORD said to Moses, "Speak to the people of Israel, and tell them to make tassels on the corners of their garments throughout their generations, and to put a cord of blue on the tassel of each corner. And it shall be a tassel for you to look at

and *remember* all the commandments of the LORD, to do them, not to follow after your own heart and your own eyes, which you are inclined to whore after. So you shall *remember* and do all my commandments, and be holy to your God." [emphasis added]

These visible symbols were to call to their *mind* His commandments so that they would not follow after their own ways. Moses repeatedly called the children of Israel to *remember*. If they started to worry about provisions, they were to *remember* that though they were slaves in Egypt, God had redeemed them with a mighty arm (Deut 5:15). If they became afraid of the nations that they were to dispossess from the land, they were to *remember* what the Lord did to Pharaoh (Deut 7.18). If they got too complacent in the land because of their prosperity, they were to *remember* that it was the Lord who gave them the power to acquire wealth (Deut 8:18). If they became self-righteous, they were to *remember* how they provoked God in the wilderness (Deut 9:7).

This same pattern is found throughout the Psalms, the hymnbook of ancient Israel. They were constantly implored to *remember* the mighty deeds of the Lord.[106] The prophets also constantly engaged the mind of Israel, recalling to them the Torah and urging them to think upon who God is and what He had done.[107] The pattern remains the same in the New Testament. Jesus instituted the Lord's Supper saying, "Do this in *remembrance* of Me" (Luke 22:19) [emphasis added]. This ordinance is to bring to our mind what Christ has secured for us in redemption. Timothy was urged to "*Remember* Jesus Christ, risen from the dead..." (2 Tim 2:8) [emphasis added]. And instead of preaching novelties, Peter described his own ministry in terms of stirring up believers "by way of *reminder*" (2 Pet 1:13) [emphasis added].

Another word analogous to remember is *consider.* In Romans 6:11 Paul said, "You also must consider (*logidzōmai*) yourselves dead to sin and alive to God in Christ Jesus." Consider means to evaluate, take

---

[106] Ps 77:11; 78:35, 42; 105:5; 106:7; 111:4, 5; 119:55; 143:5.
[107] Isa 44:21ff., 46:9ff., 64:5; Jer 51:50; Ezek 16:22; Mic 6:5; Mal 4:4.

into account, reason, or reckon. The author of Hebrews said, "Consider (*katanoeō*) Jesus, the Apostle and High Priest of our confession" (Heb 3:1). Here, consider means to take note of, observe, or contemplate. In each of these examples, the authors of Scripture seek to engage the mind, by calling back to the mind certain truths of God's Word.

Because of the enduring battle with sin, the preacher can stand behind the pulpit each Sunday with almost guaranteed certainty that many *are not thinking rightly*. Just like the all-out assault in the Garden, sin has gone after their mind. People's perspectives about life, the world, themselves, or even God have probably become skewed. From almost every venue of media we are continually bombarded with worldly philosophies and self-centered, sensual messages. As God's people meet week after week, it is imperative to remember how susceptible we are to fall into these false mental constructs.

Preaching is designed to actively re-engage the mind toward the perspective of God and His Word because as people we are apt to follow after our own hearts and eyes (Num 15:39). When was the last time you heard a sermon on how sin distorts your thinking rather than just something bad you do? Does your congregation understand that unforgiveness, bitterness, fear, anxiety, and lust are actively engaged in building false mental constructs that pervert and distort their view of life? Do Christians realize that when evil is rooted in their hearts, they are, according to Scripture, *delusional* (Eccl 9:3)?

As preachers, one of the most important questions that we can ask of every text we expound is "How does this text potentially challenge false mental constructs that my people have succumbed to?" Or more simply, "How does this text address the mind?" The application of this question to the biblical text assures relevance. No need to change your wardrobe or find a cool video clip to play. Preach to the mind; challenge the thinking; show the congregation how sin is an active force assaulting the mind. I think the pattern of addressing the mind is clearly found in Paul's letters to the churches. Most of his epistles begin with significant doctrinal propositions that are followed by ethical imperatives. This reoccurring pattern in his letters means that addressing the mind is the first prerequisite of changing behavior.

It is significant that many of Paul's letters begin with expounding upon the believer's identity and position of being "in Christ."[108] Paul *reminded* them of the work of Christ and what it meant to their life and standing before God. The problem of self-esteem is not a modern phenomenon. There is no doubt that the believers in Ephesus and Colossae and Thessalonica were struggling with self-worth. Suffering and persecution surely caused some of them to wonder if God had really accepted them or not, just like many today whose trials and tribulations really get them wondering if they are on the right track or not.

Others in the first century churches were being faced with false teaching that insinuated that certain religious rites were needed to be truly pleasing to God (like circumcision or Sabbath-keeping); just like today when most Christians default to a performance-based relationship with God. Paul knew that these Christians had to think rightly before they could behave rightly. That is why the gospel is the essential component of our preaching. Our self-esteem or worth has nothing to do with self, but Christ. Christians need Christ-esteem.

The gospel addresses our primary need: the forgiveness of sin. But as sin has been all but eradicated from our vocabulary, we have been conditioned to think that our problems are deeper and much more complex than *just* sin. Most Christians are sure that the gospel provides the way to heaven, but they have subtly been trained to believe that down here in the real world, we have more complicated matters to solve—things like broken marriages, personality disorders, manic depressions and OCDs. For these problems Christians have begun to look elsewhere. Biblical prescriptions to these issues have been marginalized and routinely viewed as overly simplistic. After all, if you are struggling with manic-depression or OCD how does *considering* yourself dead to sin and alive to God (Rom 6:11) help?

It is imperative that preachers demonstrate that the power of sin has devastating consequences upon the mind. He must be bold and uncompromising in asserting that true and lasting transformation

---

[108] Cf. Eph 1:1–14.

comes through the renewing of the mind (Rom 12:2). Preaching to the mind challenges our perspective on life. We have no need of novelty. We stir up by way of reminder. There is a huge difference between knowing and *knowing*. One knows something as a fact; the other knows something by way of application and experience. More than ever we need to reject a sermon as merely the transmitting of facts. The preacher must labor to massage the truth of God's Word deep into the mind. When the mind is transformed, behaviors change.

In any given situation we might be more culpable and less right than we think.
Page 87

Chapter Five - Self-Righteousness and Sin

People are inherently critical beings. The scathing tongue reaches politician, neighbor, co-worker, parent, preacher, spouse, boss, government, friend, and enemy alike. It is amazing how we can see with crystal clarity the stupid decision, offensive deed, arrogant attitude, or cunning motive in *other* people. Failures that are patently obvious to us in other people are, however, conveniently obscured when they are in us. Our eagle-eye quickly turns blind when it looks within. This is precisely the problem that Jesus referred to when He said, "Why do you see the speck that is in your brother's eye, but do not notice the log that is in your own eye?" (Matt 7:3). It will be helpful to know that this innate inability to perceive our own faults is rooted in sin.

Sin's distortion of the mind produces massive repercussions. It not only distorts the perceptions of life around us, it alters our perception of ourselves. This is one of the most universal and fundamental problems of mankind. We are incapable of recognizing who we really are. As Scripture asserts, "The heart is deceitful above all things, and desperately sick; *who can understand it?*" (Jer 17:9) [emphasis added]. To the Hebrew, the heart represented the core of our being, which influences everything we are and do. The biblical portrait of the heart is profoundly unflattering. Jesus likened the heart to human factory producing "evil thoughts, murder, adultery, sexual immorality, theft, false witness, slander" (Matt 15:19). From God's perspective, the heart is "deceitful above all things" (Jer 17:9); so deceitful, in fact, that it has deceived itself. The divine verdict is absolutely devastating: There is nothing more deceptive on the earth than the human heart.

Our whole world is conditioned by our distrust of other people. We have to lock our doors, and put alarms on our cars. It is why lawyers are part of one of the most lucrative professions on the planet. It is why we have long legal contracts and swear on the Bible. It is why used car salesmen are less than esteemed. What we fail to realize, however, is that it is not just *other* people we cannot trust; it is *our* heart that is deceitful above all things. We cannot trust ourselves. Proverbs 28:26 says, "Whoever trusts in his own mind is a fool." The Puritan John Owen wrote,

> There is great deceit in the dealings of men in the world; great deceit in their counsels and contrivances in reference to their affairs, private and public; great deceit in their words and actings: the world is full of deceit and fraud. But all this is nothing [compared] to the deceit that is in man's heart toward himself.[109]

The Self-Deception of Sin

The heart is inherently deceptive and deceived because it is controlled by sin. As we saw in the Garden, the essence of sin is deception. It portrays itself as something other than it is and it promises things it cannot deliver. Ever since the Fall, the human race has been beguiled by sin and ruled by its deception. Paul said, "For sin, seizing an opportunity through the commandment, deceived me and through it killed me" (Rom 7:11). Under sin, evil people go "from bad to worse, deceiving and being deceived" (2 Tim 3:13). Once possessed by sin, we fall victim to the most terrible reality: self-deception. What can be more hopeless than self-deception? What can be worse than believing your own lies? Self-deception is like carbon monoxide; its noxious fumes are subtle and imperceptible. Mired in this state of deception, the Scriptures assert that man is unable to know his true condition.

As we have already seen, Paul has personified sin, making it an active force at work within us. That power within us is aggressively engaged in the work of deception. The Scriptures are replete with warnings of sin's self-deceiving powers. A significant part of sin's deceiving powers produces the false belief that one can escape the consequences of sin. Moses described the person who knew the demands of the Law but chose to disobey them anyway as a person who acted from a deceived heart. He described that heart as a "root bearing poisonous and bitter fruit" causing one to "bless himself in his heart, saying, 'I shall be safe, though I walk in the stubbornness of my heart'" (Deut 32:18–19).

---

[109] John Owen, ed. Kelly M. Kapic and Justin Taylor, *Overcoming Sin and Temptation* (Wheaton: Crossway Books, 2006), 253.

The transgression that speaks to the wicked convinces him that he can get away with his sin. Psalm 36:1–2 says, "Transgression speaks to the wicked deep in his heart; there is no fear of God before his eyes. For he flatters himself in his own eyes that his iniquity cannot be found out and hated." Here the deception is two-fold: First, the sin can be hidden. Second, the sin is not as bad as it really is—it will not be "hated." The sinner is described as flattering himself, literally praising himself for being able to circumvent the consequences of sin. And the power of such deception breeds the fatal mistake: He does not fear God (Ps 36:1).

The New Testament is replete with warnings against the self-deception that is often associated with sin.[110] From the frequency of his appeals, it is apparent that Paul is deeply concerned that a person who lives in a state of sin could be deceived into believing that his eternal destiny was not in jeopardy. The fact that Paul addressed these warnings to the church—to professing believers—is even more sobering. Even a person who names Christ can fall prey to the deceptive powers of sin, being tricked into thinking that they can get away with their sin. The only way to combat this delusion is with the trauma of truth. As Paul wrote, "Do not be deceived: God is not mocked, for whatever one sows, that will he also reap" (Gal 6:7).

The Self-Righteousness of Sin

If we add up the evidence of sin's power to deceive and our own inherent ability to minimize and overlook our own transgressions, the conclusion of the matter is that we are all probably much worse than we realize. Or to say it another way, we think we are more *righteous* than we are. If we would mull over that statement for even a moment, it might send cold chills down our spine. In any given situation we might be more culpable and less right than we think. Could it be possible that we have been living under the deceptive powers of sin? This is one of the great ironies of sin: it actually produces self-righteousness.

---

[110] 1 Cor 6:9–10, 15:33; Gal 6:7; Eph 5:4-6; Jas 1:26; 1 John 3:7.

Back to the Garden Again

The way sin operates is first discovered in the Garden of Eden. Sin first dresses itself up and disguises its true nature. It tantalizes the senses. For Eve, eating the forbidden fruit was not a flagrant violation of God's command; it was "a delight to the eyes" and "to be desired to make one wise" (Gen 3:6). The deception of sin is so strong. It is incredible to see someone drawn to behaviors that are clearly wrong, even destructive; yet the draw of the seeming pleasure is like an irresistible magnet to their soul. However, the power of sin goes beyond the temptation. As we see in Adam and Eve, once the transgression was entered into, the next phase of sin's power became operative. Genesis 3:7 says, "Then the eyes of both were opened, and they knew that they were naked. And they sewed fig leaves together and made themselves loincloths." Filled with the shame of their guilt, their first response was to cover themselves with hastily sewn fig leaves. This was man's first attempt at self-righteousness.

Self-righteousness is one of the most insidious effects of sin's deceitfulness in our lives. Deceived by sin we become self-righteous and self-vindicating. Human nature intuitively attempts to cover up its guilt and make it look better. It is almost comical to picture Adam and Eve frantically foraging the Garden to weave together some leaves to cover their nakedness. But it is not funny; it really is sad. What were they thinking? Something in their mind compelled them to conceal their sin. Having been deceived, they were now deceiving. When God confronted Adam and Eve in their sin, how did they respond? Did they accept the guilt of their actions and own their wicked way? No. They went from self-righteousness to self-vindication.

> **God to Adam**: Have you eaten of the tree which I commanded you not to eat?
> **Adam**: Well, it was the woman whom You gave to be with me, *she* gave me fruit of the tree.
> **God to Eve**: What is this you have done?
> **Eve**: Well, it was the serpent who deceived me and I ate.

Our parents invented the blame game, and we have been playing it ever since. At times our attempts to vindicate ourselves can be as ludicrous as Aaron's when Moses confronted him about the golden calf. Aaron said he threw the gold in the fire and out popped the calf (Exod 32:24). Our propensity to cover our sin is as natural as breathing. Boston wrote,

> Who of all Adam's sons needs be taught the art of sewing fig-leaves together, to cover their nakedness? (Gen 3:7). When we have ruined ourselves, and made ourselves naked to our shame, we naturally seek to help ourselves by ourselves: many poor contrivances are employed, as silly and insignificant as Adam's fig-leaves. What pains are men at, to cover their sin from their own conscience, and to draw all the fair colours upon it that they can![111]

This is how sin works. It operates today in our lives the very same way as it did in the Garden. We can go to great lengths to maintain the charades of righteousness that cover the ugliness of our sin. To make ourselves look better, we can always blame others. One of the hallmarks of our age is not only the loss of personal responsibility but the justification of irresponsibility. The justification of irresponsibility is the natural progression of the loss of personal responsibility. Losing personal responsibility means it is not my fault; justifying irresponsibility means it is someone else's fault. It is as natural for us to swim in this cesspool of irresponsibility as it is for fish to swim in the sea.

Abandonment of personal responsibility is reaching epic proportions in American society. Increasingly it is becoming the accepted norm for government to take an ever-expanding role of responsibility over individual decisions. It may seem innocuous or even helpful that government now mandates such things as seatbelts or prohibits the use of cell phones while driving. But underlying such intervention seems to be a premise that ultimately government can protect us from ourselves. As governmental responsibility assumes an ever-expanding role in our life, we see a corresponding dependency upon government

---

[111] Boston, *Human Nature,*
http://www.reformationfiles.com/files/displaytext.php?file=boston_humannature.html (accessed 7/11/2011).

to alleviate the consequences of foolish or sinful choices. This loss of personal responsibility comes at a high price. According to the Center for Bio-Ethical Reform, 3700 babies are aborted each day in the United States.[112] These staggering numbers only affirm the lengths human nature will go to circumvent personal responsibility for its actions.

The basic structures of our society instill and reaffirm this mindset. Our public educational system instills self-esteem, not personal responsibility, as the essential quality of human life. The mental health industry has enshrined in patients a victim mentality that has perfected self-vindication to a science. And even though the physical consequences of immoral lifestyles are more than apparent, medical practitioners can rarely address the root of the problem and treat only the symptoms. The removal of personal responsibility from our collective psyche is in accordance with the work of sin. Having escaped the consequences of sin, the charade of self-righteousness can be preserved. Unfortunately, this elemental spirit of the world has seeped deeply into the mainstream of Christianity, and much of it has poured forth from the pulpit. As pastors we have to understand that straight talk about man's ultimate problem is not going to come from somewhere else. The church is the "pillar and buttress of truth (1 Tim 3:15).

An Example from the Life of David

If we let the Bible psychoanalyze us, we find that we are masters of self-righteousness. It is not a problem for some people; it is endemic to human nature. Wherever sin is present, the deceptive powers of self-righteousness will be at work. Do not think that Christians are immune to this problem. It happens in the best of saints. David, the man after God's own heart, poignantly demonstrates how the godly can succumb to the deception of sin and be blinded by its insidious righteousness. As David reflected upon how "transgression speaks to the wicked"

---

[112] The Center for Bio-Ethical Reform, "Abortion Facts" http://www.abortionno.org/Resources/fastfacts.html (accessed 11/7/2011).

(Ps 36:1), maybe he knew all too well from his experience its devious power.

David's sin is widely known. It is quite uncomfortable to think of what it must be like to have your sin preserved forever in the pages of Scripture for all to see. Yet, is not that part of the deception: that our sin can be hidden and will not be found out (Ps 36:2)? Jesus warned against hypocrisy noting that one day there would be a full disclosure. He said in Luke 12:1–3,

> Beware of the leaven of the Pharisees, which is hypocrisy. Nothing is covered up that will not be revealed, or hidden that will not be known. Therefore whatever you have said in the dark shall be heard in the light, and what you have whispered in private rooms shall be proclaimed on the housetops.

What David did in secret is now revealed to all, and it is a poignant reminder of sin's insidious powers of deception. First, David committed adultery with Bathsheba. How ironic that David's first response to his transgression is in accord with the operative power of sin in the Garden. After his one night stand, he started sewing his fig leaves together, entering into numerous elaborate schemes to cover up his infidelity (2 Sam 11:6–13). If only he could have made Uriah sleep with his wife! How he could have flattered himself "that his iniquity would not be found out and hated" (Ps 36:2)! But alas, poor David could not make it happen; Uriah just would not cooperate with his wily schemes.

David entertained sin, but soon sin would be playing David. Remember, sin breeds sin; and in accordance with this principle, David's sexual sin first bred deceit and then murder. All of this came from his heart just as Jesus had said, "For out of the heart come evil thoughts, murder, adultery, sexual immorality..." (Matt 15:19). The murder of Uriah is a horrific act, but the character and reputation of Uriah compounds the evil even further. Uriah was a man of great integrity; moreover, Uriah had gained the reputation as one of David's most trusted and faithful elite warriors (2 Sam 23:29). In the quest to vindicate himself, however, Uriah was expendable to David. So David had him killed in battle (2 Sam 11:14–24).

It was the perfect cover up and David was happy to live behind it. It is hard to imagine, but David continued in this state for at least a year or more. The Bible records that before David was confronted in his sin enough time had elapsed for Bathsheba to give birth (2 Sam 11:27). All during this time David continued to carry out his kingly functions, rendering justice in the courts, and presumably taking part in the services of the sanctuary. The fig leaves worked…for a while. Who knows how long David could have continued to function under this facade? However indefinitely David could have continued is unknown, but a reckoning was coming. The text states simply, "But the thing that David had done displeased the Lord" (2 Sam 11:27).

The kingdom might have been deceived, David might have been deceived, but God was not. I find it interesting that the very next verse, 2 Samuel 12:1, simply says, "And the Lord sent Nathan to David…" The Lord could have appeared to David personally, but He did not. He sent an emissary, a prophet, a minister of reconciliation. Nathan was commissioned by God to expose David's sin. It was a function the prophets were called to again and again in the life of Israel. Nathan approached David with a rich man/poor man story. The rich man, who had enormous flocks and herds, took from the poor man the one little lamb that was like a daughter to him and he made it a meal for his traveling guests.

On the surface Nathan's story sounds trite. I know how cute pets can be, but it was an animal; it was not murder. David could have been annoyed to be bothered by such a trivial matter. He could have lifted his hand and rendered a hefty fine on the rich man and moved on to more important kingly matters. The biblical narrative, however, seems to highlight the insanity of David's self-deception. Nathan's story should have aroused in David the guilt of his own actions, but this was not the case. Instead we see how blinded by sin David had become. When David heard the story, the text says, "Then David's anger was *greatly* kindled against the man…the man who has done this deserves to die" (2 Sam 12:5) [emphasis added]. Sin had done its perfect work, and the deception was complete. A deceived heart can see the sin of everyone else except its own. While we might be shocked at David's blindness, we should tremble at our own.

The Revival of True Righteousness

The role of preaching in the New Testament certainly comes from the tradition of Israel's prophets, and it carries with it the same solemn responsibility that Nathan had to David—to reprove and rebuke (2 Tim 4:2). As we look at the insidious effects of sin upon the soul, we discover that one of the greatest problems in the world—and in the church—is a self-righteousness that proceeds from a deceived heart. What keeps people from coming to Christ is rarely too much sin, but too much self-righteousness. Pulpits that marginalize sin can only bring a superficial healing to God's people.

Recently, a pastor's wife of a small congregation was invited to attend a divorce recovery class sponsored by a much larger church in the area. During the class, the pastor's wife observed a spirited dialogue between the participants as they exegeted their hurt and pain. Some even expressed relief of finally being able to get out of an unhappy marriage. The pastor's wife left that night with one striking observation: not one person in the room ever said anything about how they might have contributed to the breakup of their marriage. I am not suggesting by this story that blame is always equally shared or that an abusive relationship is acceptable. But it does make the profound statement that very few people are able or willing to recognize their own culpability.

In the life of the church the "sinfulness of sin" begins with the shepherds of the flock. We cannot expect the church to take sin seriously if we do not. The pursuit of holiness is one of the minister's chief ends. Sadly, it is far more common today for a preacher to be hip rather than holy. It seems that far too many pastors make more concerted efforts in choosing their outfits and eyeglasses than they do in cultivating holiness. If the seriousness of sin is ever going to take root in the American church again, it is going to require that pastors take sin seriously in their own lives first. If you look at some of the most influential preachers throughout history, one cannot escape noticing the recognition of their own inner corruption. It is hard to believe, but many of the men we deem most holy considered themselves most sinful. The historical records of their journals and letters manifest startling revelations about the apprehensions of their own sinfulness. These men understood experientially that sin was their deepest problem. The recognition of their sin drove them to Christ and to cherish the gospel. And it profoundly influenced their preaching.

I can say that reading Christian biographies has been one of the most influential elements in my Christian growth. When I was in seminary, one of my professors challenged us to pick a figure from Christian history to study and become something of a resident "expert" upon. I cannot actually recall all the reasons why, but I chose the famed Scottish preacher, Robert McCheyne. Although he died before his 30th birthday (May 21, 1813—March 25, 1843), he was one of the most passionate pastors and soul winners the world has ever known. In 1999 I was able to travel to Scotland and visit one of the primary places of his ministry, St. Peter's Church in Dundee. Peering in the windows of that hallowed structure, I reflected with a quiet reverence on his many tearful hours of praying and preaching in this place.

During my time in Scotland I visited many of the old bookstores that can be found throughout the country. In Dingwall I found a quaint little bookstore that was disorderly and seemingly insignificant. As I was digging through piles of old books, my eye caught sight of an old faded red book. As soon as it was in my hand, I knew I found a treasure. It was an original edition of Andrew Bonar's biography of McCheyne. I immediately purchased it for about $7. With its yellowed pages and brittle binding, I should probably keep it in a glass case, but I don't. I read from it again and again. It is too valuable to simply keep as a trophy. I am convinced that McCheyne's memoirs should be required reading for any man entering into the pastoral ministry. The greatest qualification of his ministry did not come from a certificate or degree; but rather, it came from his experiential knowledge of sin and redeeming grace.

One of the greatest hallmarks of McCheyne's life was his quest for godliness. He is known to have often prayed, "Lord, make me as holy as a pardoned sinner can be made." Bonar wrote, "Two things he seems never to have ceased from—the cultivation of personal holiness, and the most anxious effort to save souls."[113] It was not only the secret

---

[113] Andrew Bonar, *Memoir and Remains of the Rev. Robert Murray M'Cheyne* (Edinburgh:William Oliphant, 1874), 154.

of his power and effectiveness, but for him it was the clarion standard of any who dared to stand behind a pulpit to speak God's Word. McCheyne summed it up well saying, "The greatest need of my congregation is my own personal holiness." He believed this was an essential quality of a pastor and frequently challenged his colleagues to this standard. In a personal charge to one of his fellow ministers, McCheyne wrote:

> Lead a holy life.—I believe, brother, that you are born from above, and therefore I have confidence in God touching you, that you will be kept from the evil. *But oh! study universal holiness of life. Your whole usefulness depends on this.* Your sermon on Sabbath lasts an hour or two—your life preaches all the week. Remember, ministers are standard-bearers. Satan aims his fiery darts at them. If he can only make you a covetous minister, or a lover of pleasure, or a lover of praise, or a lover of good eating, then he has ruined your ministry forever. Ah! let him preach on for fifty years, he will never do me any harm. Dear brother, cast yourself at the feet of Christ, implore his Spirit to make you a holy man. Take heed to thyself and to thy doctrine.[114] [emphasis added]

One of the most needful things in the 21st century church is a true revival among the pastors and elders of the church of Jesus Christ. The quest for godliness and the power of a holy life is the prerequisite of preaching. This is not a Puritan methodology; it is Pauline. McCheyne understood it well. Paul told Timothy, "Keep a close watch on yourself and on the teaching. Persist in this, for by so doing you will save both yourself and your hearers" (1 Tim 4:16). As preachers, so much more is involved than just being able to deliver a good sermon. Our ministry requires that we first take sin seriously in our own lives and doggedly pursue righteousness. After we have kept a close watch on ourselves, then comes the careful attention to our preaching—"*keep a close watch on yourself and on the teaching.*" Carefully note that salvation is the product of such a union: "You will save both yourself and your hearers" (1 Tim 4:16b). Clearly, the preacher's personal life is instrumental in his corporate ministry.

---

[114] Ibid., 362.

The corollary of a man's personal life to his ministerial effectiveness produces a sobering thought for the preacher: over time your congregation will spiritually look like you. If you are a hypocrite, your people will be hypocrites. If you have closet sins, they will have closet sins. If you love the gospel and pursue holiness, they will love the gospel and pursue holiness. Preaching is so much more than a sermon, and there is so much at stake. God has ordained this office to accomplish eternally significant purposes. As McCheyne wrote, "It is not great talents God blesses so much as great likeness to Jesus. A holy minister is an awful weapon in the hand of God."[115]

---

[115] Bonar, *Memoirs,* 241–2.

> *Man's real problem*
> *is his free will.*
> Page 106

Chapter Six - The Will and Sin

Several years ago the Kansas City Chiefs, my hometown NFL team, garnered a coveted Monday night game on primetime television. The whole city buzzed with excitement. As the fortunate ones with tickets made their way to the stadium, they snarled traffic for all the unfortunate ones who just wanted to get home. As often happens in Kansas City, the weather did not cooperate that night. It was downright dreadful. Torrential rains blanketed the stadium and soaked everybody in it. It rained so hard at times that water was literally flowing down the aisles like a river. Let me tell you, it was a great night to watch the game...in your living room. The scene that night broadcast on TV was something to behold. There were about eighty thousand fans packed into Arrowhead Stadium getting totally soaked, but they cheered enthusiastically throughout the entire game. Most of the fans were forced to stand the whole game, even if for no other reason than to see over the umbrellas in front of them.

The game finally finished around 11 p.m., but the debacle was not over yet. The weather, combined with a mass of humanity trying to exit one place at the same time, created a traffic nightmare that kept people from getting home until the wee hours of the morning. On top of all that, I am sure that many of them had to get up early Tuesday morning for work. What a fiasco; but do you know what was *really* crazy? The fans seemed to love it. No one *had* to be there; they *wanted* to be there. The rain only seemed to bring out the "fanatic" in the fan. In a sports-crazed world, such behavior is more common than strange. People will endure all sorts of inconvenience and expense to enjoy their athletics. As for other forms of entertainment, it is not uncommon to drop a hundred dollars or so for a night out on the town.

However, an odd thing happens when you take the same time and money spent on our entertainments and invest them into the church and the things of God. All of a sudden our economy of time and money and energy undergoes a strange transformation. The same people who would *pay* to sit through a two or three hour movie will squirm when the sermon goes over 15-20 minutes long. The hours that fly by in the theater suddenly become the longest hours of the day in a worship service. The hundred-dollar bill that seems like nothing on a Friday night becomes a precipitous mountain in the offering plate on Sunday morning. The zeal to sit outside in pouring down rain for Monday Night football mysteriously evaporates when it comes to venturing out to church when it *looks* like it might rain. It is a strange phenomenon, right?

The Corruption of the Will

The riddle is solved. The answer is *sin*. Sin has captured the will and brought it under its power. The will is a comprehensive term that references the things a person wants or desires; it dictates the things that we love or hate. Anthony Hoekema wrote, "What we call 'the will,' however, is simply another name for the total person in the act of making decisions."[116] The radical transformation in the economies of our time and money and energy comes from sin. Our wills are inclined towards pleasure and entertainments but predisposed against God and things of God. It is ironic that the church has been embroiled in contentious battles over the will for centuries, because God's verdict on the human will is devastatingly clear all throughout Scripture. As Marguerite Shuster said, "Scripture uses almost unbelievably strong figures to emphasize our moral impotence."[117] According to Scripture, there is none who seek after God; everyone has turned aside to their own way (Ps 14:2-4; Isa 53:6; Rom 3:11). "Not seeking God" corresponds directly to the will: man does not *want* to seek God but instead, prefers to pursue his own interests. Likewise, Isaiah declared, "There is no one who calls upon your name, who rouses himself to take hold of you" (Isa 63:7). Somewhere deep in the heart of man is an inability or unwillingness to expend the necessary energy to grasp hold of God.

The corruption of the will is uncontested in the New Testament. In John 3:19 the verdict against the world is that "the light has come into the world, and people *loved* the darkness rather than the light because

---

[116] Anthony Hoekema, *Created in God's Image* (Grand Rapids: Eerdmans Publishing, 1986),171.
[117] Marguerite Shuster, *The Fall and Sin* (Grand Rapids: Eerdmans Publishing, 2004), 185.

their deeds were evil" [emphasis added]. The things that we love, the affections of our will, are predisposed toward darkness and not light. The New Testament also makes clear that heredity plays a key role in these dark inclinations, and it goes beyond our biological parents. It goes even beyond our first parents—Adam and Eve. According to Scripture the parentage that ultimately determines the will is spiritual, whether you are a child of God or a child of the devil (1 John 3:10). Accordingly, Jesus said of the Pharisees, "You are of your father the devil, and your *will* is to do your father's desires" (John 8:44) [emphasis added]. To be children of the devil is to have the same predispositions as the devil.

Years ago a popular comedian, Flip Wilson, popularized the phrase, "The devil made me do it" in his comedy routines. As a child, I can fondly remember my brother and me playing his hilarious monologues over and over again on our vinyl record player. We laughed so hard it hurt. Admittedly, Flip Wilson never claimed to be a theologian, but it is tempting to make the devil a convenient scapegoat for our own peccadillos. The Bible, however, does not let us off quite so easily. According to James, "Each person is tempted when he is lured and *enticed by his own desire"* (Jas 1:14) [emphasis added]. According to James, it is not the devil who lures and entices us; it is *our own will.* John Owen wrote, "Temptation and occasions put nothing into a man, but only draw out what was in him before."[118] James pictures the will as a determinative force within us. The word "lure" in the Greek is a strong word; it literally means to be dragged away. According to Peter Davids the word "entice*"* (*exselko*) "suggests a fish being drawn out of the water by a line."[119] With the use of a passive participle, James portrays the whole course of our life being directed by the force of our will. Thus, our actions and behaviors are ultimately dictated by our will.

The nature of the will is clearly complex and the notion of a "free will" is a theological freight train that has been debated for well over a millennium and a half in the church. In his book, *The Freedom of the*

---

[118] Owen, *Overcoming Sin and Temptation*, 250.
[119] Peter Davids, *Commentary on James,* New International Greek Commentary (Grand Rapids: Eerdmans Publishing, 1982), 84.

Will, Jonathan Edwards asserted, "It is easy to see, how the decision of most of the points in controversy, between Calvinists and Arminians, depends on the determination of this grand article concerning the freedom of the Will [sic]..."[120] For some, free will is a *sine qua non* of Christian thought to avow at all cost. From this perspective, the affirmation of free will is an integral part of a theodicy (a defense of God). It is assumed that if the will is not free, then God must be the ultimate author of sin, an idea interestingly enough, that James absolutely repudiates in the previous verse. "Let no one say when he is tempted, 'I am being tempted by God,' for God cannot be tempted with evil, and He Himself tempts no one' (Jas 1:13). No, according to James, our *will* is the culprit that tempts us (Jas 1:14).

The Ultimate Problem of the Will

The corrupted will is a massive problem for man. The apostle Paul reminded the Ephesians of their pre-conversion condition by stating, "And you were dead in your trespasses and sins..." (Eph 2:1). "Dead" is a fairly stringent word. O'Brien wrote that it "denotes a state of alienation or separation from God."[121] When we consider the word "dead" there isn't a lot of wiggle room for a definition. Paul used the Greek word *nekros* which is commonly defined in Greek lexicons as "that which refers to a corpse." You can poke a corpse, push it, or even scream at a corpse, but it will not respond and cannot perform any functions. It is obvious that Paul must be using this term metaphorically—or at least spiritually—since Paul knew the Ephesians had to be very much alive before they were saved, at least physically. According to Paul, they were *walking* according to "the course of this world" (Eph 2:2) and *lived* "in the passions of our flesh, carrying out the desires of the mind" (Eph 2:3). It is interesting, the word *desires* in Greek is *thelēmata,* the will. Even though dead, their will was very much alive. Anthony Hoekema wrote,

---

[120] Jonathan Edwards, *The Freedom of the Will* (Vancouver: Eremitical Press, 2009), 266.
[121] O'Brien, *The Letter to the Ephesians,* 156.

> The fact that human beings have now lost true freedom does not mean that they have lost the ability to make choices. They now sin willingly, choosing to do so. They still make choices, but the wrong ones. They are now under the bondage of sin.[122]

As we work to understand what Paul means by being "dead" yet physically alive, we can deduce that Paul must be referring to *spiritual* death amidst physical life. Surely, the echoes of the Fall found in Genesis 2:17 can clearly be heard, "for in the day that you eat of it you shall surely die." Although Adam did not immediately die physically, in order for Scripture to be true, he must have died *spiritually* the very moment of his rebellion. At that instant, sin accomplished a *coup d'etat* over the mind and will of man. His ability to save himself, his will to seek after God, was gone. He was *spiritually dead*. This spiritual death is operative among all unconverted humanity, because from the moment of the Fall and beyond, the divine verdict upon humanity is that there are *none* who seek after God; they have *all* gone their own way. In the case of the Ephesians, they were physically alive and their will was actively functioning as it carried out the desires of the mind. Thus, "being dead in trespasses and sins," must mean at the very least that certain components of the will and intellect had been rendered inoperative by sin and unable to perform any functions.

A truly "free" will, therefore, runs counter to the teaching of Scripture. Proverbs 5:22 says, "The iniquities of the wicked ensnare him, and he is held fast in the cords of his sin." Jesus taught that whoever commits sin is a slave of sin (John 8:34). Paul referred to unredeemed humanity as being "enslaved to sin" (Rom 6:6), "slaves to impurity and to lawlessness" (Rom 6:19), and "slaves to various passions and pleasures" (Titus 3:3). This is all in accordance to the dire warning of God found in the Garden: the moment that you eat, sin will take all of you; you will die. Throughout Scripture there is a comprehensive unity on this subject; yet various factions within the church have been embroiled in a battle over the nature of the will for centuries. Why is that? Perhaps the most compelling reason is that arguing against a "free" will runs contrary to our experience. We are rational beings who exercise choice all the time. We aren't robots. No one has to sin, we

---

[122] Hoekema, *Created in God's Image*, 233.

choose to sin. Many times those who argue against free will leave the unmistakable impression that humans are nothing more than pieces on a chessboard whose actions have been elaborately predetermined. God is the master puppeteer, pulling all our strings.

But such conclusions run completely contrary to Scripture. As already noted, James emphatically asserts that God tempts no one with evil (Jas 1:13). Man is tempted and lured to evil by his own will (Jas 1:14). In fact, all throughout Scripture, responsibility for sin always falls squarely on the shoulder of the sinner. The Bible plainly asserts that God is not the author of sin, but He is sovereign over it. One of the more remarkable examples can be found in the calamities that befell Job. When the Lord allowed Job to fall into the hands of Satan, the first assault came from the Sabeans, who plundered his livestock (Job 1:15). Since Scripture asserts that God does not tempt with evil, we can't conclude that God made the Sabeans attack Job. James Beck wrote, "Significantly, God can move the human will without violating freedom."[123] It is safe to assume that the marauding Sabeans had been eyeing Job's livestock for some time. In fact, the book of Job states that God had put a hedge of protection around Job and his possessions (Job 1:10). There is no doubt that God's protection of Job had, heretofore, thwarted the Sabeans' evil desires and intentions. To demonstrate how God is sovereign but separate from sin, all God had to do was lift His sovereign hedge of protection, and the Sabeans became free to do that which they had wanted to do for a long time. Thus, we see in Scripture that man's will can be restricted by God and it can be allowed free reign; but in every circumstance it is always under the sovereign plan and purpose of God.

In this scenario it is obvious that the notion of free will is not quite so simple. The Sabeans were not totally free to do as they pleased because God restrained them from attacking Job. Yet, when they attacked Job, God was not dictating their deeds; they were acting upon their own desires. When it comes to understanding the will of the natural man similar complexities can be found. Frankly, I believe that

---

[123] James Beck, *The Human Person in Theology and Psychology* (Grand Rapids: Kregel Publications, 2005), 225.

"free will" is an unfortunate term that brings with it a tremendous amount of theological baggage. Martin Luther seemed to agree. He wrote, "I wish the word 'free will' had never been invented. It is not in the Scriptures, and it were better to call it 'self-will,' which profiteth not."[124] Unfortunately, however, denying the concept of free will may cause significant confusion. Instead of *denying* free will, it seems more judicious to me to *clarify* it like Luther did. In one sense, the will has to be free or it is no longer the will. If I do something against my will, I would be doing something under compulsion, not freedom. John Owen wrote, "Every sin is so voluntary, that if it be not voluntary, it is not sin."[125] In Scripture, man is not condemned for acting under compulsion, but rather for acting "according to the *will* of his flesh" (Eph 2.3) [emphasis added].

So how can we clarify the notion of free will? First of all we can assert that man is clearly a *volitional* creature. What does volitional mean? According to the dictionary, volition is the act of making a choice or decision.[126] In many ways volition is synonymous to willpower. James Beck wrote, "Volition is the capacity for self-determination or the freedom to be who I am."[127] Thus, man is a volitional creature in that he has a power of will which is formative in decision-making. In spite of all the theological battles concerning the will, the biblical evidence clearly demonstrates that man's volition—his power of will—has been thoroughly corrupted by sin. He still has the power of will, but that will is dominated by sin. That is the essence of Paul's verdict rendered upon the status of the pre-converted Ephesians.

Paul explains the concept of being dead in sin as living a life (i.e. "walking") that follows certain patterns. The pre-converted Ephesians made decisions in their life that followed the "course of this world" (Eph 2:2); that is, they lived their life just like everyone else did. But as Paul laid out the indictment, following the course of this world is to follow a more sinister pattern: the pattern of "the prince of the power

---

[124] Hugh Thomson Kerr, Jr., ed., *A Compend of Luther's Theology* (Philadelphia: Westminster Press, 1943), 91.
[125] Owen, *Overcoming Sin*, 333.
[126] http://www.merriam-webster.com/dictionary/volition (accessed 5/4/2012).
[127] Beck, *The Human Person in Theology and Psychology*, 224.

of the air, the spirit that is now at work in the sons of disobedience" (Eph 2:2). O'Brien wrote, "Here the word designates the spirit's evil supernatural activity whereby he exercises a powerful, compelling influence over the lives of men and women."[128] So when people are doing the things that they want to do, they are actually following what *Satan* wants to do. There is a striking corollary here to the confrontation Jesus had with the antagonistic religious leaders of Israel when He stated, "You are of your father the devil, and your will is to do your father's desires" (John 8:44). In Paul's worldview, the pre-converted Ephesians were under the same indictment as the Christ-rejecting Pharisees, whose will was to do Satan's desires. That is what it means to be "dead in your trespasses and sins."

Ultimately, when we talk about free will we must understand that the will is free only in the sense that it carries out its own desires. Free will does not mean that we can do whatever we want to do. A few years ago "I Believe I can Fly" was a popular song. Some of us can still hear the chorus ringing in our heads,

> *I believe I can fly,*
> *I believe I can touch the sky*
> *I think about it every night and day*
> *Spread my wings and fly away*
> *I believe I can soar*
> *I see me running through that open door*
> *I believe I can fly, I believe I can fly, I believe I can fly*[129]

It was a catchy tune but it is utterly ridiculous. It does not matter how much you may want to spread your wings and fly away; it is not going to happen. Free will obviously has its limits.

If we are going to clarify the notion of free will, we cannot deny the volitional character of man, nor should we go on tirades against free will. Rather we can confidently show that man's real problem *is his free will,* or in the words of Luther, "self-will." His will has been corrupted by sin and in freedom all his wants and desires are inclined

---

[128] O'Brien, *The Letter to the Ephesians*, 161.
[129] "I Believe I Can Fly," (Epic Records 1996) Kelly, R.

towards evil. In Paul's letters to the churches, the activities of unredeemed humanity are continually characterized as being in the state of carrying out the "desires of the flesh and the mind" (Eph 2:3, NAS). Man is corrupted through their "deceitful desires" (Eph 4:22), and living only to "gratify" the desires of the flesh (Rom 13:14). Indeed, for Paul, living how you want to—according to the *will* of the flesh—is one of the defining characteristics of the unregenerate.[130] According to Paul, the "desires of the flesh are against the Spirit" (Gal 5:17).

One of the more sobering judgments in Scripture is found when God throws off His restraint and gives men over to the sinful will of their flesh. Romans 1:24 says, "Therefore God gave them up in the lusts of their hearts to impurity, to the dishonoring of their bodies." In verse 26, God gives them up to "dishonorable passions" which results in all kinds of gratuitous sin. Charles Hodge wrote, "The moral degradation of the heathen was a punishment of their apostacy [sic] from God."[131] Getting away with sin may seem like freedom, but in reality it is judgment. Like the Sabeans, when God lets men do what they want to do, they give themselves over to do evil. Again, our problem, according to Scripture, is our will. The whole way of life is "corrupt through deceitful desires" (Eph 4:22).

This is why Boston wrote, "There is in the unrenewed will an aversion to good. Sin is the natural man's element…He is a captive, a prisoner, and a slave, but he loves his conqueror…"[132] With a corrupt will the things of God are burdensome, boring, and foolish. It is why children can play video games for hours but have to be cajoled to go to church. It is why a $100 bill seems like nothing on a Friday night but a veritable mountain in the offering plate. The inclinations of the heart are bent towards our own pleasures rather than the will of God. For decades churches have been trying to attract the "unchurched." Maybe we should ask why these people are "unchurched." The underlying

---

[130] Gal 5:16–7; 5:24; Eph 2:3; Col 3:5.
[131] Charles Hodge, *Commentary on the Epistle to the Romans* (1886; repr., Grand Rapids: Eerdmans Publishing, 1994), 42.
[132] Boston, *Human Nature,* http://www.gracegems.org/28/human_nature.htm (accessed 6/12/2011).

assumption has been that it has been the fault of churches. It is argued that our methods are archaic, our services are boring, and our message is offensive. Sadly, it has been almost completely forgotten or overlooked that the trouble might not be with the church at all, but with the "unchurched" themselves.

The will is one of the soul's most accurate spiritual barometers, and understanding the nature of the will corrupted by sin is paramount to the ministry of preaching. It is significant that a corrupted will is, according to Paul, equivalent to being "dead." The only hope to this predicament is to be "made alive" (Eph 2:5) or "born again" (John 3:3) or "regenerated" (Titus 3:5). This supernatural power is found only in the gospel, which is the "power of God to salvation" (Rom 1:16). Those who are touched by its power are deemed "new creation" in which "the old has passed away; the new has come" (2 Cor 5:17). Under the power of the Holy Spirit the will is made alive and transformed. Things people once loved are now hated; and things once hated are now loved. In rejecting the biblical verdict on the will, many church leaders have stooped to the employment of carnal and worldly tactics to resuscitate the dead. We have attempted to make the church fun and entertaining. It is commonplace for youth group leaders to install flat screen TVs and video gaming stations to entice teens to their services. Among adults, the new fad is for pastors to incorporate movie clips into their sermons so as to keep the attention of the congregation. However, flat screen TVs, gaming stations, and movie clips cannot raise the dead.

Some will argue that these are merely tools to attract people to the church so that they will hear the truth. Pragmatically, it sounds like wise advice, but pragmatism is not the guiding force of our methodology; God's Word is. Paul's methodology is scandalous to our pragmatic age because Paul flatly refuted any human contrivances that would rob the transformation of sinners from the glory of God's power. He wrote,

> And I, when I came to you, brothers, did not come proclaiming to you the testimony of God with lofty speech or wisdom. For I decided to know nothing among you except Jesus Christ and him crucified. And I was with you in weakness and in fear and

much trembling, and my speech and my message were not in plausible words of wisdom, but in demonstration of the Spirit and of power that your faith might not rest in the wisdom of men but in the power of God (1 Cor 2:1-4).

Hodge wrote, "Paul relied, therefore, for success, not on his skill in argument or persuasion, nor upon any of the resources of human wisdom, but on the testimony which the Spirit bore to the truth."[133]

The Only Prescription for the Will

More than ever before the church needs to recover its confidence in the gospel. The most pressing need is not to make the message palatable but plain. The prophetic mantle of preaching is truth-telling. Paul declared, "For I am not ashamed of the gospel for it is the power of God to salvation…" (Rom 1:16). We need to rescue Paul's assertion of the gospel's power from the rubbish pile of familiarity. We are not ashamed of the gospel when we have the conviction that the transforming power of God is at work in the simple but profound proclamation of the crucified Christ. When we look to other methods to help accomplish the work of salvation, confidence in the gospel is jeopardized. The danger of being ashamed of the gospel comes when we encounter people who reject the gospel as offensive or simply ignore it because it is boring. Paul was in prison because of the rejection of the gospel, but he was never embarrassed about its power.

While studying the book of Luke I was amazed at the preaching style of John the Baptist. Luke wrote, "He said to the *crowds* that came out to be baptized by him, 'You brood of vipers! Who warned you to flee from the wrath to come?'" (Luke 3:7) [emphasis added]. Calling the crowds a brood of vipers is not very seeker-sensitive. Matthew records that John said these words when he saw *many* of the Pharisees and Sadducees coming for baptism (Matt 3:7). If we put these two accounts together, I get the distinct impression that although the Pharisees and Sadducees must have incited those stern words from John, it was said in such a way that if you were in that crowd you

---

[133] Charles Hodge, *Commentary on the First Epistle to the Corinthians* (1950, repr., Grand Rapids: Eerdmans Publishing, 1994), 32.

would have assumed John was talking to you. That is why Luke said, "He said to the *crowds*..."

It is astounding to think that at this point in the drama of redemption *many* Pharisees and Sadducees were standing in line for baptism; but this is the last time in the Gospels that the Jewish religious leaders will respond in *en masse* to the message of truth. In fact, from this point on the Pharisees will become the chief antagonists of Christ. It is highly probable that John's severe indictment was the initial catalyst of their ultimate rejection. They must have been thoroughly offended by John's stern words. In light of John's preaching, it is a wonder that *anybody* stayed around for baptism. Yet many were baptized by John. The message that drove the Pharisees away, drew many others, among whom were Andrew and Peter who soon would follow the Lord Jesus Christ (John 1:35-41). Paul's ministry followed a similar pattern of plain truth-telling that drove away and drew. He declared that his message is "folly" to those who are perishing (1 Cor 1:18); and it was a stumbling block to the Jews and foolishness to the Gentiles (1 Cor 1:23). However, to those whom God was calling it was the "power of God" (1 Cor 1:24). The truth, even when it is hard, finds an ear among those who are called.

Any attempt to embellish the gospel is a declaration of embarrassment. We have to come to grips with the fact that in our own power we cannot make people interested in the truth. Pragmatically speaking, preaching the message of truth will not always "work" or yield the outcomes that we want. It might not result in a mega church; but it will result in the true church. That is why Paul treasured the gospel and labored to guard it from embellishment. He labored tirelessly for its advancement throughout the Roman Empire.

The ministry of reconciliation is a distinguishing ministry. The message of truth divides those who hear it. It winnows the threshing floor by separating the wheat from the chaff (Luke 3:17). Jesus Christ, the Prince of all Preachers, never attempted to attract the masses. In fact, He often avoided drawing a crowd, and His ministry was met with more rejection than reception. His stated goal was to call sinners to repentance (Luke 5:32) and to gather into one the children of God who are scattered abroad (John 11:52). The distinguishing power of the message is evidenced in one of the fiercest debates Jesus had with His adversaries, He said to them, "You do not believe because you are not of My sheep" (John 10:26). Those are striking words. He did not say they were not His sheep because they did not believe; but they did not believe *because* they were not His sheep. Then Jesus said, "My sheep hear My voice…and they follow Me" (John 10:27). We cannot entertain dead men to life, but we can preach to them the words of eternal life.

Today, some have erected a tombstone over preaching because it no longer works.[134] Maybe they are right; but even if they are, Paul has a sobering command: "Preach the word; be ready in season and out of season" (2 Tim 4:2). The words "be ready" could literally (and perhaps more accurately) be translated "stand by or near." Thus, Timothy is urged to stand by or remain committed to preaching the Word in the good times and the bad. Today may very well be an "out of season" time for preaching, but a faithful minister doesn't have another option. As shepherds of the flock, ministers are called God's stewards (Titus 1:7); and it is required of stewards that they be faithful, not necessarily successful (1 Cor 4:2).

---

[134] Pagitt, *Preaching Re-Imagined*, 18.

> *Biological factors do not invalidate one's responsibility toward righteousness.*
>
> Page 133

Chapter Seven - The Body and Sin

Since our culture has become adept in eradicating sin from our vocabulary, the consequences of sin are routinely misdiagnosed. One day while driving around town during the Thanksgiving season I listened to a local Christian radio station. People called the station to publicly express their "attitude of gratitude." One man who called said that he had been struggling with alcoholism for years and wanted to give thanks for his eleven days of sobriety. After the radio announcer celebrated with him and encouraged him in his struggle, the caller concluded with a rather off-handed remark saying, "After all, alcoholism is a disease."

His comment stuck in my mind like an arrow. What did he mean alcoholism is a disease? There is no doubt that alcohol has significant influence upon the body's biology; but was his behavior rooted in physiological abnormalities? Was a virus or bacteria causing him to abuse alcohol? There has been a growing assumption that alcoholism may have some sort of genetic connection, especially since a child of an alcoholic is four times more likely than other children to become an alcoholic. But as one popular internet resource on alcoholism pointed out, an actual gene has yet to be identified that causes alcoholism.[135] No one can be sure if the statistics concerning children of alcoholics are anecdotal or if environmental factors may be a significant factor. However, even if an actual "alcoholic" gene could be identified, would personal responsibility be abated? The answer is no. The alcoholic can never be placed in the same category as the victim of cancer, because drinking alcohol is a volitional choice; it is a matter of the will. Cancer is not.

If we diagnose drunkenness as a disease, what is adultery? Should we search for an "adultery" gene in the philandering husband? There is no doubt that physiological components are integral to sexual attraction. Hormones have an inherent correlation with sexual desire, but the raging hormones that inflame midnight dalliances in porn or illicit

---

[135] Buddy T. "Alcoholism—Is it Inherited?," http://alcoholism.about.com/cs/genetics/a/aa990517.htm (accessed 11/29/11).

affairs cannot rightly be classified as "diseased." It really does not matter if science discovered a gene behind habitual lying, cheating, stealing, or a host of other aberrant behaviors, because even if physiological factors affect our behaviors, the Bible still calls it sin. What became evident about this particular caller was that he had been culturally (if not religiously) trained to treat his inherent sinful behavior as a biological or organic problem, not a spiritual one. Calling drunkenness a disease is a misdiagnosis.

The Complexity of the Issue

There is clearly a mysterious relationship between the body and soul, and in this chapter we must address a very complex and easily misunderstood issue. In all my years of pastoring, no issue has garnered more response and aroused more irritation than when I speak on the issue of how sin affects the body. Explanations as to how sin affects the body run from one extreme to another. One extreme can be illustrated by the response of Job's friends to his suffering and physical ailments. Eliphaz, Bildad, and Zophar were confident that Job's troubles (presumably even the boils he scraped with broken pieces of pottery) were all caused by his own wickedness. They would soon learn a very humbling lesson. The other extreme is easily demonstrated in our own day and age by psychologists, medical doctors, educators, and religious leaders who would never assert (at least publicly) that sin was a root cause of illness. To them such an admission would be horrifying.

The complexity of the issue is exemplified by the scourge of AIDS that is ravaging many parts of the world. On one hand, only a small degree of intellectual honesty would admit that AIDS, like other sexually transmitted diseases, is the consequence of sinful sexual behaviors. Even the Centers for Disease Control and Prevention acknowledges that "Many young people engage in sexual risk behaviors that can result in unintended health outcomes."[136] Thus, it is

---

[136] Centers for Disease Control and Prevention, "Sexual Risk Behavior: HIV, STD, & Teen Pregnancy Prevention," http://www.cdc.gov/HealthyYouth/sexualbehaviors (accessed 8/27/11).

obvious even to health care practitioners that persons who engage in sexual immorality (a word they admittedly would not use) run a greater risk of contracting certain diseases than others. But even a disease like AIDS cannot be always tied directly to sinful behavior.

In 2009 it was reported that over twenty-two million people were living with HIV in sub-Saharan Africa.[137] Of that number, over two million are children, and that does not include the almost fourteen million children who have been orphaned because of AIDS.[138] Most of those children infected with HIV are so because of a parent, not their own sexual behaviors, and millions of orphans are suffering consequences not of their own making. These are just a few of the realities that make this subject so complex.

When Christians assert that sin affects the body, we are entering into a very mystical and mysterious field that even the most educated medical experts among us are only beginning to discover and understand. Ultimately we are exploring how the body and soul are intimately integrated; how the material and the immaterial are assimilated into one organic whole. That there *is* a relationship between the body and soul, the material and immaterial, is one of the great complex and mysterious phenomena of life. Beck wrote, "Within the unity of the human person, the physical body functions harmoniously with the mind, volition, emotions, desires, and moral sense."[139] While complex and mysterious, it should nonetheless be abundantly clear that there is a definite connection between the two. When someone gets the flu or suffers from severe migraines, it has a profound effect on that person's spirit. Physically sick people often become dispirited, weak, and discouraged. Conversely, an afflicted spirit makes an intense impact on the physical body.

Emotional distress can be a significant detriment to the physical well-being of a person. Beck wrote that "Ninety percent of all suicides are connected to psychopathological and/or substance/alcohol abuse."[140]

---

[137] Avert, "Sub-Saharan Africa HIV & AIDS Statistics," http://www.avert.org/africa-hiv-aids-statistics.htm (accessed 8/27/11).
[138] Ibid.
[139] Beck, *The Human Person in Theology and Psychology*, 228.
[140] Ibid., 96.

Recently, a family in our congregation had to face a horrible ordeal when their eighteen year old nephew committed suicide. By all outward appearances he was a normal young man with a bright future. Even though we do not need experts to tell us this, research has established that depression and feelings of hopelessness have been found to be closely related to suicide risk. One journal of psychiatry even noted that "research has found that hopelessness and extreme pessimism about the future have a strong association with suicidal tendencies."[141] Considering that, according to the National Institute of Mental Health, suicide was the third leading cause of death for young people ages 15 to 24,[142] identifying the problem is a critical issue. These are startling statistics and the realization that the emotional/spiritual well-being of the soul has a profound impact upon the overall physical well-being of the person should inspire all ministers of the gospel to take this issue very seriously.

There is a fine line between the body and soul, and that line is often blurred as we do not always understand the interaction between these two entities. We must be careful to avoid resorting to a radical dualism that treats these entities as two entirely different aspects of our being, because they are not. The mind and the brain are not the same thing. Clearly they are integral to an organic whole, yet they are also distinct. There is a profound difference between a brain soaking in a jar of formaldehyde and a brain nicely connected in the skull of a functioning human. Though distinct, the mind and the brain are intimately connected to each other in a way in which each has a profound influence upon the other.

While rejecting a rigid dualism, we must also be diligent to acknowledge the distinction. We live in an age in which health care (physiological treatment) and mental health care (psychological treatment) are being subtly merged into one science. Dr. Matthew

---

[141] James C Overholser, Stacy R Freiheit, and Julia M DiFilippo, "Emotional Distress and Substance Abuse as Risk Factors for Suicide Attempts," *Canadian Journal of Psychiatry* 42, no. 4 (May 1997): 402.

[142] National Institute of Mental Health, "Suicide in the U.S.: Statistics and Prevention," http://www.nimh.nih.gov/health/publications/suicide-in-the-us-statistics-and-prevention/index.shtml (accessed 11/21/2011).

Stanford, professor of psychology at Baylor University, lists the basis (or biological predisposition) of sinful behavior as one of the main three points of conflict between science and religious belief.[143] Mental health experts are making radical attempts to sweep all abnormal psychological, emotional, and addictive behaviors into physiological categories. But as Beck wrote,

> When scientists attempt to utilize an extreme materialism to explain everything about the human person, they are taking great, unsupported leaps of logic across a span of problems that demand a better set of explanations.[144]

Recently, in an article entitled "Addiction is a brain disease, experts declare," the Los Angeles Times reported that the American Society of Addiction Medicine asserted that "Addiction is not simply a behavioral problem involving too much alcohol, drugs, gambling or sex…Addiction is a primary, chronic disease of brain reward, motivation, memory and related circuitry."[145]

The implicit conclusion to these presuppositions is clear. As Tyler and Grady state, "This interpretation views man as a victim who is sick rather than a sinner who is responsible to God."[146] Furthermore, it squeezes the minister and the gospel out of the solution. It is true that a pastor, unless he has been trained otherwise, is not a medical doctor, and his knowledge of physiological matters is limited. He should always approach this subject with a heavy dose of caution and humility. Yet, it is not hard to see how a preacher can be intimidated by the conversations and arguments of the academic elite. Becoming conversant in these matters may be very helpful to the pastor, but let us not forget that the ultimate qualifications of our ministry are found in two very important places: A holy life and mastery of the biblical text (1 Tim 3:1–7; 4:15–6). With these credentials we can proclaim without intimidation, "Thus says the Lord…" We are not required to have a

---

[143] Matthew Stanford, *Biology of Sin: Grace, Hope, and Healing for Those Who Feel Trapped* (Colorado Springs, CO: Biblica Publishing, 2010), 10.
[144] Beck, *The Human Person in Theology and Psychology*, 174.
[145] Rosie Mestel, "Addiction is a Brain Disease, Experts declare," *Los Angeles Times*, August 16, 2011.
[146] Tyler and Grady, *Deceptive Diagnosis,* 2

mastery of all the sciences. As guardians and purveyors of the "deposit of truth," we possess in the Word of God an infallible and authoritative diagnosis of the human condition. It is our calling to underscore the divine proclamation to a world that is lost and in rebellion to their Creator.

We live in a day that desperately needs a wise and compassionate courage in the pulpit. I am convinced that we are rapidly approaching the moment when faithfulness to God's Word, especially in matters like this, is going to require us to be willing to sacrifice our reputation. It may result in being ridiculed as fools, ignorant, or judgmental. If so, we stand in the noble tradition of an apostle who described himself and his co-workers as "a spectacle to the world…like the scum of the world, the refuse of all things" (1 Cor 4:9, 13). When you consider that down through the history of the church, faithfulness to the message often meant martyrdom, ridicule is a small price to pay.

The Physiological Effects of Sin

As we have examined the effects of sin thus far, we have seen that sin is a malignant power that affects the mind and the will—all elements of the immaterial part of our being. Scripture, however, is unquestionably clear that sin also affects the physical body. Historically, the church has affirmed this truth. Four hundred years ago, Thomas Watson wrote, "Sin turns the body into a hospital. It causes fevers, ulcers, and apoplexy."[147] Only recently has this conviction been questioned. The first (and worst) universal effect of sin upon the body is death. In the Garden, it was the first pronounced consequence—"for in the day that you eat of it you shall surely die" (Gen 2:17). The violation of God's command causes death. It was the penalty enshrined in the Law of God (Deut 24:16); and the prophets of Israel reiterated the divine verdict (Jer 31:30; Ezek 18:20). In the New Testament the apostle Paul referred to death as "the wages of sin" (Rom 6:23). Those who work iniquity get paid with death. According to Paul, the universal reality of death is squarely pinned to the

---

[147] Watson, *The Mischief of Sin*, 6.

universal presence of sin (Rom 5:12). Thus, the spiritual presence of sin results in the physical death of all humanity.

But the malignant power of sin that affects the immaterial part of man also affects the material part of man even beyond the penalty of death. Scripture speaks of sin corrupting the body. Quoting from the Old Testament, Paul wrote, "Their **throat** is an open grave; they use their **tongues** to deceive. The venom of asps is under their **lips**. Their **mouth** is full of curses and bitterness. Their **feet** are swift to shed blood" (Rom 3:13-15) [emphasis added]. A few chapters later Paul warned believers not to allow the members of their body to be "instruments" of sin (Rom 6:13). The word "instrument" is *hoplon* in Greek. It refers to a weapon or tool. Thus, we are not to let our bodies be a tool that sin uses. In these verses, Paul views sin as materially affecting members of the body, especially those involved in communication (throat, tongues, lips, and mouth).

Two Principles

Beyond being a tool of sin, our body can bear other physical manifestations of sin's presence. Before we consider the physical effects of sin upon the body, there are two very important principles that we must keep in mind. These two principles correspond to the two types of sin: Original sin and Actual sin. Original sin (sometimes called Ancestral sin) infects the whole human race (Ps 51:5) and all of creation (Rom 8:23). It was passed down to us from our father Adam. Original sin denotes the presence of sin but not necessarily the act of sin. Actual sin, as implied in the name, refers to the act of sin itself. It is any attitude or behavior that is perpetrated against the law of God, like lust, gluttony, greed, sloth, wrath, envy, and pride. In addressing the subject of sin affecting the body, one has to determine whether the sin is Original or Actual.

Indirect Consequences

The first principle for us to establish is that sin is indirectly related to all sickness, suffering, and death. The word indirectly is the key. All the suffering and death in the world is related to sin generally though not always specifically. This first principle corresponds to Original sin. The presence of sin brought about a curse on the world that encompasses all pain and illness and sorrow and suffering. In some way, sin, by divine fiat, opened the door for tragedy in life, breaking down the human genetic code making the body susceptible to disease, sickness, and ultimately death. What this means is that all suffering and death are at least indirectly related to the reality of sin in the human race.

Although all suffering and tragedy and disease can be traced back to the presence of sin, not all suffering and tragedy and disease can be attributed to a particular sin. Numerous biblical texts assert this very important principle. The story of Job profoundly illustrates it. Job's suffering and misery was not related to his sin. Job's friends made the lethal error of assuming otherwise. Their narrow worldview assumed that all misery and misfortune were directly related to specific sins. Ironically, this was a worldview that Jesus' own disciples shared. When they encountered a blind man they asked Jesus, "Rabbi, who sinned, this man or his parents, that he was born blind" (John 9:2)? Jesus answered, "It was not that this man sinned, or his parents, but that the works of God might be displayed in him" (v. 3). Specific or actual sin was not the cause of this man's blindness. This man was born into a sin cursed world with blindness, and his blindness would serve to show the redemptive purposes of God.

As expert caretakers of the soul, the preacher must always be cognizant that not all sickness and bodily suffering is the direct result of sin. A dear brother and fellow elder in our church has a body racked with Rheumatoid arthritis. This is a wretched disease that inflicts pain in almost every joint in his body, distorting his fingers and making him a virtual prisoner in his own body. But this man has been a devoted and exemplary believer most of his adult life. His disease, though part of a sin cursed world, is not directly related to a specific sin. His fortitude and grace in bearing this cross has been an inspiration to all those around him.

When we look at the indirect consequences of Original sin in our world, there is no cure in this life. Eventually death and illness of one sort or another will prevail. Our bodies, indeed the whole earth, groan for our redemption (Rom 8:23). The only cure to these ills will be in the New Heaven and Earth when sin is ultimately removed from all of creation. When preachers encounter those suffering under the indirect consequences of sins which abound in our world, they must point them to the gospel and the promise of eternal life, the only balm to a transient and sin cursed world.

Direct Consequences

The second principle we must establish corresponds to Actual sin in which suffering, sickness, and death can be directly attributed to specific sinful behaviors. Though obvious, this principle has the potential to be an explosive assertion. From this principle, the Bible teaches that when people actively engage in sinful behaviors the result can be sickness or suffering, and may, in fact, hasten the day of their death. Sometimes the physical effects of sin on the body are as obvious as personal appearances. A person can look like they have lived a "hard life." I remember several years ago when a homeless man came to our church asking for money. The smell of alcohol was prominent on his breath. His hair was gray, his face was worn and wrinkled, and most of his front teeth were missing. I figured the man to be well into his sixties. I was astounded when he told me he was forty-eight years old. Hard living had taken its toll.

Throughout Scripture there is a direct correlation between behaviors and physical consequences. Quoting from Psalms, the apostle Peter wrote, "Whoever desires to love life and see good days, let him keep his tongue from evil and his lips from speaking deceit; let him turn away from evil and do good" (1 Pet 3:10–11). Proverbs says that the fear of the Lord and the turning away from evil "will be healing to your flesh and refreshment to your bones" (Prov 3:7–8). Conversely the Bible warns that foolish, sinful behaviors have physical, even bodily, consequences. For example the Bible warns of the physical consequences of sexual immorality. Solomon pleads with his son to avoid it because at the end of his life "you will groan when your *flesh and body* are consumed" (Prov 5:11) [emphasis added]. More poignantly Solomon warns, "He who commits adultery lacks sense; he who does it destroys himself" (Prov 6:32). Romans 1:26-27 contains an explicit warning against homosexual behaviors. Paul states categorically that those who engage in such a lifestyle receive "in themselves the due penalty for their error" (Rom 1:27). The correspondence of the AIDS epidemic among the homosexual community suggests to many that this disease may in fact be part of that judgment.

In the Old Testament, Israel was warned that disobedience against the covenant would result in the Lord striking them with "wasting disease and with fever, inflammation and fiery heat…" (Deut 28:22). Correspondingly, in the New Testament there are similar warnings. The celebration of the New Covenant during the Lord's Supper requires believers to examine and judge themselves (1 Cor 11:28–9). This examination and judgment is the process of dealing with sin in one's life. According to Paul, it was imperative to understand this because those who did not were "weak and ill, and some have died" (1 Cor 11:30).

The Bible and our experience substantiate the fact that sinful behavior affects the physical body. The evidence is so patently obvious that to argue against it is foolish. For instance, it is medically established that sustained abuse of alcohol (what the Bible calls drunkenness) can cause liver disease. The physical effects upon the body from using Methamphetamine are staggering. Methamphetamine destroys dopamine receptors in the brain and over time literally changes the brain's chemistry. It has been proven that cocaine radically increases heart rate and blood pressure while simultaneously constricting the arteries supplying blood to the heart, many times resulting in a heart attack even among people without heart disease. Gluttony has been linked to Type 2 diabetes. And sexual immorality, as already noted, can cause a litany of sexually transmitted diseases.

It is fascinating to consider that it is not necessarily the substance or even the behavior itself that causes the negative consequences. It is the *sin* that wreaks havoc on the body. Michael Mangis wrote, "Sin involves directing something good toward a use which violates God's purpose for it."[148] There are studies that suggest moderate consumption of some types of alcohol may be beneficial. The ingredients used to make Methamphetamine are found in some

---

[148] Michael Mangis, *Signature Sins, Taming Our Wayward Hearts* (Downers Grove, IL: IVP Books, 2008), 41.

medicines that can relieve symptoms of the common cold. Consider the fact that a man and woman can enjoy decades of sexual intimacy in the bonds of marriage and never once have to worry about contracting a STD. Thus, it is not necessarily the substance or the act that results in destructive physical consequences, but the sin. The violation of God's law will result in the body being adversely affected.

Psychosomatic Illnesses

If sinful behaviors affect the body, what about sinful *thoughts?* Is it possible that the metaphysical act of *thinking* can result in adverse physical consequences? Again, the evidence seems to overwhelming support such a conclusion. Beck wrote, "Behaviors impact the mind, and the mind directs behaviors. Feelings direct behaviors, and behaviors shape feelings."[149] Mental health practitioners have long recognized that bodily ailments can be caused by mental or emotional disturbances. These disturbances have been termed "Psychosomatic." In his book, *From Paralysis to Fatigue,* Edward Shorter defines a psychosomatic illness as "any illness in which physical symptoms, produced by the actions of the unconscious mind, are defined by the individual as evidence of an organic disease and for which medical help is sought."[150] In layman's terms, a psychosomatic illness is an illness in the body caused by disturbances in the mind. It should be noted that even though these illnesses originate from the mind, there is nothing imaginary about the illness. The pain is not "just in their head." The physical consequence of an emotional disturbance is real.

Numerous studies reveal this link. There is research to indicate that intense periods of stress can be a contributing factor to stomach ulcers.[151] And one popular medical resource on the web warns that high levels of anger have been linked to heart disease.[152] Moreover, we

---

[149] Beck, *The Human Person in Theology and Psychology*, 229.
[150] Edward Shorter, *From Paralysis to Fatigue: A History of Psychosomatic Illness in the Modern Era* (New York: The Free Press, 1992), x.
[151] Ulcer-Cure, "What is the main cause of an ulcer?," http://www.ulcer-cure.com/Ulcer_Symptoms/cause-of-an-ulcer.php (accessed 10/21/11).
[152] Katherine Kam, "How Anger Hurts Your Heart," http://www.webmd.com/balance/stress-management/features/how-anger-hurts-your-heart (accessed 10/21/2011).

know that anxiety can commonly cause things like indigestion or spastic colons. If we know that these metaphysical acts can affect the biology of the body, is it possible that lust, greed, guilt, or bitterness could also have an effect upon the body and chemistry of the brain?

Ironically, it has become increasingly normal to treat emotional disorders from a biological rather than spiritual perspective. People seeking help for anger or worry or other severe mental disorders are routinely being prescribed psychotropic drugs without addressing what has caused the emotional disturbance in the first place. A number of years ago a young woman came to me for counseling. Her life was full of all sorts of troubling circumstances. Her marriage was rocky, her job had been incredibly stressful, and her relationship with her parents had been rapidly deteriorating. She had been unable to sleep and was suffering with severe bouts of depression. When she went to the doctor she was diagnosed as manic-depressive with a chemical imbalance and given a prescription for medication.

As the young woman shared with me the story of her woes, I asked her if she had told the doctor about the difficult circumstances of her life. She replied that she had not. As I visited with this young woman my heart went out to her. I asked her, "Do you think there might be a correlation between your depression and the circumstances you are going through?" She answered quietly, "Yes." Then I shared the obvious with her. "Do you realize," I asked, "that there isn't a pill in the world that can change your circumstances?" She knew there wasn't. The medications may have numbed her feelings, but it did nothing to alter the cause of her condition. Robert Smith M.D., an author and believer, made this startling admission about his own profession, "It is far easier and quicker for the medical profession to dispense a pill than deal with the reasons for the pills being used."[153] Ultimately, her problem was an unbiblical response to life's circumstances, and the only remedy was repentance and renewed faith in the care and provision of her God in the distresses of her life. By the

---

[153] Robert Smith, M.D., *The Christian Counselor's Medical Desk Reference* (Stanley, NC: Timeless Texts, 2000), 73.

power of the Holy Spirit she did not have to be a slave of her circumstances.

The use of psychiatric medications is an immense subject that would be difficult to cover in a book, let alone one chapter. A recent article from Fox News reported that 20% of Americans use psychiatric drugs.[154] The same article stated that in 2010, "Americans spent $16.1 billion on antipsychotics to treat depression, bipolar disorder and schizophrenia, $11.6 billion on antidepressants and $7.2 billion on treatment for ADHD, according to IMS Health, which tracks prescription drug sales."[155] These staggering numbers will probably continue to rise as counselors and medical practitioners continue to rely more and more upon pharmaceuticals to relieve the symptoms of emotional turmoil and trauma. Every Christian pastor needs to be prepared to face this crisis.

The role of prescribing psychiatric medications is a contentious debate even among Christians. Michael Mangis is a professor of psychology at Wheaton College, a practicing psychologist, and author of *Signature Sins, Taming Our Wayward Hearts*. Even as a psychologist, Mangis writes with a pastor's heart. Although our solutions are profoundly different in many places, I believe Mangis confronts the problem of sin in *Signature Sins* with a candor that I have come to appreciate.

In a chapter entitled "The Biology of Sin," Mangis describes a counseling session with a young woman that I believe deserves further scrutiny as an important test case. Mangis wrote,

> One young woman, referred to me by her pastor, told a story that truly astounded me. After years of infertility, she had become pregnant but then experienced a miscarriage. Due to complications from the miscarriage she had to have a hysterectomy, which threw her into immediate menopause and ended her hopes for children. The surgery led to complications that required her to go under the knife, under general

---

[154] http://www.foxnews.com/health/2011/11/17/one-in-five-american-adults-takes-psychiatric-drugs/ [accessed 1/24/12].
[155] Ibid.

> anesthesia, two more times. She was normally a cheerful and energetic young woman known for her positive outlook and willingness to help anyone in need. Now she was severely depressed, struggling to get out of bed in the morning. She felt lethargic and hopeless. She received no pleasure in anything. She even found it difficult to pray or attend church. Nevertheless she was praying diligently for healing, as were her husband and members of their church.
>
> When I asked this woman why she had not gone to her physician to ask about antidepressants, she replied that she and her husband believed that her problem was a spiritual issue. If she prayed with enough faith, God would heal her. With encouragement and education about a Christian view of medications, this woman was able to receive help from a physician in the form of an antidepressant medication.[156]

As heart-rending as this story is, it isn't an isolated event. Mangis is not playing unfairly by employing some extreme encounter. Behind the Sunday morning smile, these are the kinds of tragedies and heartaches in the congregation that pastors will face each week.

For Mangis this was a situation that necessitated antidepressant medication. In fact, Mangis asserted that Christians' resistance to the use of psychiatric medications is a "contemporary form of the ancient heresy of the Gnostics."[157] He asserted that Christians who resist such medications adopt a form of Gnosticism, because in his words "they believe supernatural forms of healing are superior to biological forms of healing."[158] He even goes so far as to say that refusal to consider taking an antidepressant "could be a sin."[159] These are very strong statements that need to be answered.

---

[156] Michael Mangis, *Signature Sins: Taming Our Wayward Hearts* (Downers Grove, IL: InterVarsiy Press, 2008), 131.
[157] Mangis, *Signature Sins,* 132.
[158] Ibid.
[159] Ibid.

One of the first things that must be recognized is Mangis' flawed terminology. To suggest that the resistance to these medications is on the grounds of spiritual vs. biological forms of healing is disingenuous at best. There is no correspondence between psychiatric medications and healing. In fact, no psychiatric drug on the market would ever claim to heal anything, and as a psychologist, Mangis would know that. This is not an issue of supernatural forms of healing verses biological forms of healing; and those who oppose prescribing or taking psychiatric medications do not use those grounds. Because Mangis framed this encounter in these flawed constructs, his diagnosis of the problem and solution are apt to be flawed as well.

Furthermore, considering several significant phrases this young woman used, it is striking that Mangis would first question why this young woman had not yet consulted a physician for antidepressants without much further investigation. Why was she severely depressed? Was it from the complications of the hysterectomy or the fact that her hopes and dreams of motherhood were traumatically ripped from her soul? She stated that both she and her husband believed that her problem was a spiritual issue. What did she mean by that? Was she struggling with anger, disappointment, or resentment toward God? Surely the sentiment "If she prayed with enough faith, God would heal her" would stimulate further investigation. Does she have a biblical understanding of prayer, faith, or suffering? These are extremely significant issues that if explored from a biblical context could have yielded profound insight and perhaps even healing.

Sadly, the tragedy of this young woman is not an isolated event. This kind of suffering and affliction has been the destiny of God's people down through the ages. I have been with young couples who lost their infant children, wives who have lost their godly husbands, and others who have faced prolonged seasons of excruciating pain from terminal illnesses, not to mention those who suddenly lose a job or have faced extended periods of unemployment. In each case these believers are faced with profound questions about God's purpose and plan for their life, not to mention His goodness and love toward them. It is not uncommon for those who go through such intense afflictions to also have to endure many dark nights of the soul. Depression, discouragement, and even despair are common assaults upon the souls of these precious saints. If the crushing loss of the dream of motherhood is not a significant factor in this young woman's severe depression, she would certainly be in a minority.

The preacher has a profound role in ministering to people like this. One of the most important things that a preacher can do is to preach to his congregation in a way that prepares them *before* suffering and tribulation befall. Sermons that promote a "best life now" will profoundly fail to equip believers for the heart-rending trials that they will most certainly face. This was one of the defining characteristics of Paul's ministry to established churches. Acts 14:22 says that when Paul and Barnabas returned to the believers in the cities of Lystra, Iconium, and Antioch, they were "strengthening the souls of the disciples, encouraging them to continue in the faith, and saying that through many tribulations we must enter the kingdom of God." Likewise, Peter equipped believers for suffering by demonstrating that trials are unique opportunities to test the genuineness of faith (1 Pet 1:6–7). James went so far as to even say that believers should "Count it all joy…when you meet trials of various kinds," because "the testing of your faith produces steadfastness" (Jas 1:2–3). Trials are instrumental in proving our salvation. James wrote, "Blessed is the man who remains steadfast under trial, for when he has stood the test he will receive the crown of life" (Jas 1:12).

This incident also underscores the necessity of a gospel-centered ministry. The gospel is the only true balm to an afflicted soul. The gospel alone removes the enmity of God from us, and it radically alters how we view our trials. Many Christians have to endure circumstances of "dark providence," and often those circumstances cause us to question God's love toward us. The Scriptures, however, remind us that our circumstances (no matter how difficult they may be) are not the ultimate indicator of God's disposition towards us. The cross is the ultimate indicator. Paul said in Romans 8:31–32, "What then shall we say to these things? If God is for us, who can be against us? He who did not spare his own Son but gave him up for us all, how will he not also with him graciously give us all things?" No amount of tribulation or distress can separate us from that love (v. 35). When the guilt of our sin has been removed by the blood of Christ, our trials are not retributive but redemptive. Jeremiah Burroughs wrote, "Thus, affliction is nothing to them who have no guilt…"[160]

Assured of our reconciliation, there is only one thing left for the follower of Christ to do when grievous trials are encountered. Peter wrote, "Humble yourselves, therefore, under the mighty hand of God so that at the proper time He may exalt you, casting all your anxieties on Him, because He cares for you" (1 Pet 5:6–7). Mind you, this was written to a group of believers who were "exiles of the dispersion" (1 Pet 1:1). These were people who had been driven from their homes and livelihoods. They were faced with uncertain and terrifying prospects in foreign lands; but they were called to humble themselves under God's mighty hand. In these verses, Peter not only assured them of God's ultimate sovereignty over their lives, but also of His unfailing care and concern for them. As shepherds of God's flock, it is incumbent upon pastors to remind God's people of His faithfulness and the importance of trusting Him with a childlike simplicity.

The realization that sinful behaviors and thoughts can physically affect the body has profound implications upon the pastoral ministry. The preacher must exercise great wisdom in diagnosing human ills. He must be cognizant of the fact that not all illness or affliction is directly related to sin. In fact there are instances when biological causes may, indeed, contribute to aberrant emotions and behaviors. For example, diabetes, hysterectomies, or high blood pressure can profoundly affect the body and the mind. It is always good to encourage people to get a medical examination if they are experiencing unexplained emotions or behaviors. However, there are also times when the preacher must have the courage to point out where sin—unbiblical responses to life's circumstances in thought or deeds—is the root problem. He must be cognizant to the fact that, as Smith pointed out, "Sin cursed people want a reason for behavior that removes personal responsibility—the illness label provides this escape."[161]

---

[160] Burroughs, *The Evil of Evils*, 138.
[161] Smith, *The Christian Counselor's Medical Desk Reference*, 50.

Biological Behaviors

The overwhelming trend today is to attribute biological causes to sinful behaviors. We are told that explosive anger, severe depression, and extreme mood swings are the result of chemical imbalances in the brain and should be treated with various pharmaceuticals. According to an article in Time Magazine, antidepressant use in the U.S. doubled in the years from 1996 to 2005, resulting in over twenty-seven million people using antidepressants in America.[162] Efforts to attribute sinful behaviors to biological causes are also being made in the matter of human sexuality. Homosexuality is increasingly explained as a condition someone is born with. The controversy obviously has a profound effect on how we address these conditions. It is assumed that if behaviors are rooted in biological abnormalities, then the treatment of such people should be placed in the hands of doctors not pastors.

As Christians I think we need to ask ourselves, "What if it could be scientifically proven beyond a shadow of a doubt that such behaviors are indeed biologically based?" How should the church respond if it is, in fact, discovered that an improper brain chemistry results in rage or severe depression? How should we respond if research could identify beyond a shadow of doubt a homosexual gene? Would it sideline the church? Would it render the gospel any less effective? In processing questions like this, I believe we need to consider several important matters.

First, we should ask ourselves how we would respond to a man who physically abused his wife, but claimed to have a genetic predisposition to anger. Would that justify his behavior? Of course not. Even if someone has a biological or genetic predisposition to an aberrant behavior, it is still unacceptable (i.e. wrong) to act upon it. According to Scripture there is no excuse for sin. In fact, God demands obedience even when one is biologically predisposed to act another

---

[162] Alex Altman, "Antidepressants in America," *Time Magazine,* August 5, 2009.

way. For example, the scriptural standard of moral purity is specifically applied to young men whose hormones inflame their sexual passions.[163] Biological factors do not invalidate one's responsibility toward righteousness. The Bible teaches personal responsibility for all our behaviors.

Secondly, a biological basis for sinful behaviors would only confirm, not deny, the witness of Scripture. The Bible asserts that man is born sinful. The natural inclinations of humanity are bent toward iniquity. We are natural born liars and cheaters and inherently selfish. My parents never had to teach me any of those things. Though unlikely, if it could be clinically proven that a person is born with a "homosexual" gene—or any other sin gene—it would not undermine the testimony of Scripture, only affirm it.

The massive attempts today to transform sin into sickness should not surprise us. Escaping personal responsibility is something handed down to us from our parents in the Garden. All along the Bible has asserted that our problem is sin. Perhaps more than any other time in the history of the world, it will fall upon the preacher to recover the fact that when you engage in sinful thoughts or behaviors you are harming your body and its physiological functions, perhaps in ways that we have yet to discover. In this day and age the diagnosis of sin will only come from the church. When behaviors and attitudes that do not conform to the law of God are discovered, they need to be called what they are: sin. In reclaiming the diagnosis of sin, the church also recovers the only true remedy: the gospel.

Our treasure is the gospel. It is the power of God to salvation. It changes people. It transformed the brain chemistry of a man named Saul in such a way that he went from a hater of Jesus to His most ardent lover and apostle. We can contextualize this whole issue if we look at Paul's letter written to the church at Corinth almost two thousand years ago, and substitute his vocabulary with the words that are being used today. In today's vernacular 1 Corinthians 6:9-10 might read something like this:

---

[163] See Prov 5; 6:24–33; 7:5–23; 9:13–8.

> Do not be deceived: neither [people with a hyperactive sexual disorder], nor [the co-dependent], nor [the one who has affairs], nor [the one who suffers with alcohol dependence], nor [the one who practices an alternative lifestyle], nor [the kleptomaniac], nor [the one with a compulsive buying disorder], nor [the one with an oppositional defiant disorder], nor [the pathological liar] will inherit the kingdom of God.

As Paul surveyed the Corinthian church these were the very kinds of people he saw; but there was something different about them. Again, he wrote, "And such were some of you. But you were washed, you were sanctified, you were justified in the name of the Lord Jesus Christ and by the Spirit of our God" (1 Cor 6:11). The behaviors and attitudes that had previously defined them and barred them from the kingdom had been washed away by the blood of Jesus Christ. If sin can have such a profound effect upon the biology of the body, I have a growing confidence that the gospel does as well. That means the gospel of Jesus transforms us in ways we may have never perceived. As Paul proclaimed, "If anyone is in Christ, he is a new creation. The old has passed away; behold, the new has come" (2 Cor 5:17).

*Sin ravages
relationships.*
Page 140

Chapter Eight - Relationships and Sin

Hopefully by now you have begun to see that sin is something so much greater than just wrong that we do. The presence of sin is toxic and it permeates our whole being—body and soul. Every path of sin leads to deceit and destruction. The effects of sin on the mind, the will, and the body are inevitable, even if oftentimes subtle. When sin hardens the will and builds false constructs in the mind, people often do not realize they are operating under the influence and power of sin. They simply continue to carry on deceiving and being deceived. And although sin can cause mental disorders, aberrant and addictive behaviors, and numerous diseases, it is rarely considered the culprit.

In this chapter we are going to explore another area that sin affects—*profoundly*. The effects of sin in this area are probably felt more acutely, more universally, more cognizantly than any other area of our life. We see these effects everywhere around us. From its very inception at the beginning of time throughout the course of history to this very day sin has literally ravaged *relationships*. Sin distorts and destroys relationships. Beck wrote, "An accurate indicator of the condition of the human heart is the nature of our relationships—how we interact with and respond to others, especially those closest to us."[164] According to Scripture, the destructive nature of sin in relationships is manifested in three primary areas: our relationship to the earth; our relationship to others; and most importantly, our relationship to God.

Our Relationship to the Earth

Fifty years ago it would probably have seemed odd to write a book on the subject of sin and bring up the subject of environmentalism; but fifty years ago green was only a color. Today, ecology is one the major issues facing the Church, as concern for the environment has taken on epic proportions. As a philosophy, environmentalism has become an entrenched part of the educational system, the global political culture,

---

[164] Beck, *The Human Person in Theology and Psychology*, 322.

the movie industry, and even in the Church. If environmentalism primarily referred to a good stewardship of our natural resources, there would be little need to address it. Environmentalism, however, has moved far beyond good stewardship of the earth's resources. In many ways, environmentalism has become a global religion. According to an article in the *The New Atlantis, A Journal of Technology & Society*, "For some individuals and societies, the role of religion seems increasingly to be filled by environmentalism."[165] The article included a fascinating quote from a climate change skeptic, Michael Crichton, who asserted that environmentalism has remapped Judeo-Christian beliefs. According to Crichton,

> There's an initial Eden, a paradise, a state of grace and unity with nature, there's a fall from grace into a state of pollution as a result of eating from the tree of knowledge, and as a result of our actions there is a judgment day coming for us all. We are all energy sinners, doomed to die, unless we seek salvation, which is now called sustainability. Sustainability is salvation in the church of the environment. Just as organic food is its communion, that pesticide-free wafer that the right people with the right beliefs, imbibe.[166]

Sadly, this pseudo-religion has made its way into the church. Numerous evangelical leaders are championing the environmental cause; and in many Christian institutions, ecology has subtly replaced theology. Recently, *The New York Times* reported that many churches are looking to the environmental cause to bolster their sagging attendance and connect with their community. Whereas churches once went into the neighborhood to preach the gospel, now churches are going door-to-door to promote environmental concerns. The article in *The New York Times* quoted a pastor from Spokane, Washington who frequently employs such environmental campaigns as saying, "I've never been good at door-to-door evangelism, but this has been so fun. Everybody wants to talk to you. It's exciting. It's ministry."[167]

---

[165] http://www.thenewatlantis.com/publications/environmentalism-as-religion (accessed 1/6/2012).
[166] Ibid.
[167] William Yardley, "Pastors in Northwest Focus in 'Green'," *New York Times Religion Journal*, January 15, 2010.

While many well-meaning Christians are actively involved in environmental issues, many of them are woefully ignorant of the underlying premises of the movement that are blatantly unbiblical. Climate change advocates assert that a significant cause behind natural disasters (like floods, drought, famine, hurricanes, and tornados) is climate change. The changes in the earth's climate are said to be the result of manmade pollutants and general mismanagement of the earth's resources. In short, the culture has undergone a massive paradigm shift in which the spiritual worldview found in Scripture has been replaced with an ecological worldview. In an ecological worldview, natural disasters are rooted in the ecological mismanagement of the earth's resources. The Scriptures, however, assert that our planet was placed under a curse because of our sin, and the environment has been reeling under sin's reign ever since. Moo wrote, "Humanity's fall into sin marred the 'goodness' of God's creation, and creation has ever since been in a state of 'frustration'."[168]

The problems with our environment originated in the Garden of Eden. When Adam and Eve sinned, God placed a curse on the earth. Genesis 3:17-19 says,

> And to Adam [God] said, "Because you have listened to the voice of your wife and have eaten of the tree of which I commanded you, 'You shall not eat of it,' *cursed is the ground because of you*; in pain you shall eat of it all the days of your life; thorns and thistles it shall bring forth for you; and you shall eat the plants of the field." [emphasis added]

Clearly, man is responsible for the condition we find on the earth. As the Lord said, "cursed is the ground *because of you...*" The curse, however, was for sin not ecological mismanagement. In the New Testament Paul described the curse as the earth being "subjected to futility" (Rom 8:20), and that the "whole creation has been groaning together in the pains of childbirth until now" (Rom 8:22).

While the merits of environmentalism and climate change are being debated in some scientific circles, it is incumbent upon faithful

---

[168] Moo, *The Epistle to the Romans*, 514.

ministers of the gospel to have the courage to stand up and assert that the problem facing the planet is not pollution but sin. Israel's prophets consistently linked environmental consequences to sinful behaviors. One of the curses for disobedience to the *Torah* would be drought. Moses said, "The heavens over your head shall be bronze, and the earth under you iron. The Lord will make the rain of your land powder. From heaven dust shall come down on you until you are destroyed" (Deut 28:23-24). And through the prophet Isaiah, the Lord declared,

> The earth lies defiled under its inhabitants; for they have transgressed the laws, violated the statutes, broken the everlasting covenant. Therefore a curse devours the earth, and its inhabitants suffer for their guilt; therefore the inhabitants of the earth are scorched, and few men are left. (Isa 24:5-6)

And Jeremiah described the land as "mourning" under the wickedness of its inhabitants (Jer 12:4).

It is time to realize that environmental issues are not the sole property of the scientific community. Because of its prominence today, the preacher has a unique opportunity to address these issues from a biblical framework. Exposing the environmental agenda will not be a pleasant task, but it is mandatory if we are going to be faithful to the biblical message. The ultimate cause of natural disasters is not our carbon footprint; it is our rebellion against our Creator. Famine, drought, and catastrophic phenomenon indicate that something is wrong.

Paul wrote, "For the wrath of God is revealed from heaven against all ungodliness and unrighteousness of men who suppress the truth in unrighteousness" (Rom 1:18). Have you ever wondered how the wrath of God is revealed from heaven? Paul was a Jew whose worldview was shaped by the Old Testament. As a Christian, he would recoil in horror at the notion of "Mother Earth." There can be no doubt that in Paul's mind natural disasters must be one way in which the wrath of God is revealed from heaven. Paul knew that in wrath the world was once destroyed by a flood. Sodom and Gomorrah were reduced to ashes by fire and brimstone, and plagues and pestilence decimated the land of Egypt.

While shocking to modern sensibilities, the Old Testament is replete with the knowledge that God is the Architect of disaster. When a whirlwind destroyed the house and his children in it, Job responded, "The Lord gave and the Lord has taken away" (Job 1:21). Psalm 29 ascribes to the Lord the glory found in thunder (v. 3) and wind (v. 5) and lightning (v. 7) and earthquakes (v. 8). According to Jeremiah, the God who created the sun and fixed the order of the moon and the stars is the same God who "stirs up the sea so that its waves roar" (Jer 31:35). The prophet Amos declares plainly, "Does disaster come to a city, unless the LORD has done it? (Amos 3:6). And dare we mention how God is going to bring history to an end? In the final displays of His wrath against all ungodliness and unrighteousness, God is going to pour out on the earth famine, drought, pestilence, and earthquakes unlike anything the world has ever seen before (Rev 6).

The disasters that fall upon the world demand an explanation and interpretation. Pollution and the squandering of the earth's resources are the interpretation of the environmentalists not the biblicist. Natural disasters remind us that something is terribly wrong in our world. Jesus described these disasters as "the beginning of the birth pains" (Matt 24:8). They are mere harbingers of a greater disaster looming over humanity.

It would be imprudent to assert that natural disasters are always directly related to a *specific* sin of a *specific* people. In the wake of the tsunami of 2004 in Southeast Asia that killed over 200,000 people, some Christian leaders implied that this area in Southeast Asia was specifically targeted for disaster because it represented an area of the world that persecutes Christians the most.[169] While those facts may be true, they also overlook the fact that many churches were destroyed and numbers of believers were also killed. Here in the Midwest, tornados that destroy churches are just as likely to destroy bars. In the devastating earthquake and tsunami in 2011 in Japan, both the Seaside

---

[169] Ken Camp, "Blackaby says tsunamis God's judgment; mission's experts question theology," *Associated Baptist Press*, January 26, 2005.

Bible Church and the pastor's home were completely destroyed.[170] Only the foundation of the church was left. Jesus Himself gave the most cognizant response to any natural disaster. Instead of linking the disaster to the sins of the victims, Jesus made the poignant point, "Unless you repent, you will all likewise perish" (Luke 13:3).

Natural disasters not only demonstrate God's wrath against *all* ungodliness and unrighteousness, but serve as powerful evangelistic opportunities that force people to come to grips with their own rebellion and sin against God. The Christian minister must be able to articulate a gospel-orientated explanation and response to the demonstration of God's wrath in the wake of natural disasters. The wholesale embracement of the environmental movement abdicates the opportunity we have to explain the broken relationship that sin has caused in our world.

Our Relationship to Others

Beyond ruining our relationship to the earth, sin also destroys our relationship to each other. Again, when we go back to Eden, one of the first consequences of sin manifested in the Garden was the entrance of conflict into the marriage relationship. In almost cryptic language, the Lord informed Eve that because of her sin "your desire shall be for your husband, and he shall rule over you" (Gen 3:16). Scholars debate the actual meaning of this phrase, but it seems to imply that once sin entered the world, it created a power struggle between the husband and the wife. One of the most plausible meanings is that the woman will desire to control her husband, but he will want to dominate her instead. That is, in fact, exactly how the NET Bible translates that particular phrase: "You will want to control your husband, but he will dominate you." The first relationship that sin distorted was marriage.

Because sin is so self-serving, it will always create conflict with our fellow man. Sin ravages relationships. Every broken relationship is a

---

[170] Lucille Talusan, "After Japan Quake, Church Finds New Purpose," http://www.cbn.com/cbnnews/world/2011/June/After-Japan-Quake-Pastor-Finds-New-Purpose/ (accessed 10/10/2012).

result of sin, so there is no such thing as a "No Fault Divorce." Every divorce, every dysfunctional family, every feud, every conflict is always rooted in sin. It is bad enough that sin affects us in profound ways—our mind, our wills, our bodies; but it never stops with us. Our sin affects other people and how we relate to them. Many times the broken relationship is unintentional. We do not set out to destroy those closest to us, but broken relationships are always a product of sin. When a husband and wife divorce, they do not intend to harm their children; but they do. When a husband watches pornography, he generally does not set out to harm his relationship with his wife; but he does. His sin destroys the intimacy and trust of his spouse; it hardens his heart and callouses his mind, and distorts his thinking.

Since the presence of sin effects how we think, it builds those false constructs in our mind which can be devastating to personal relationships. Anger, jealousy, lust, bitterness or an unforgiving spirit create mental constructs through which we view and interpret the attitudes and actions of those around us. Through these distorted lenses intimate relationships are always in jeopardy. When a person becomes embittered towards another, every act—no matter how seemingly genuine—is suspect. And because sin is self-vindicating and produces self-righteousness, reconciliation is hindered as we blame others and refuse to take responsibility for our own actions.

Building meaningful relationships always takes work, but since sin is self-serving, opportunities to develop intimacy are jettisoned for carnal pursuits. We don't usually view sins like covetousness, or the love of money, or selfish ambition as relational sins; but each of these can play a significant role in undermining our relationships with other people. How many families have been adversely affected because the "bread winner" of the family spent more time winning bread than developing relationships in the home? It is interesting that of all God's laws that relate to our interactions with other people—like not stealing, or not murdering, or not bearing false witness—can all be summed up in the command to love our neighbor. Paul said, "For the whole law is fulfilled in one word: 'You shall love your neighbor as yourself'" (Gal 5:14).

Other sins that are often considered personal in nature, like sexual immorality or drunkenness or drug abuse, also significantly contribute to the demise of relationships with other people. Research has shown that alcohol abuse increases the rate of poor communication, violence, and feelings of distress; all of which raise the risk of divorce. Some evidence shows that divorced or separated individuals are three times more likely to be alcoholic or have an alcohol problem than married individuals.[171] But research aside, the Scriptures assert that the root of all conflict in relationships is sin. James wrote, "What causes quarrels and what causes fights among you? Is it not this, that your passions are at war within you?" (Jas 4:1).

Have you ever examined carefully the "deeds of the flesh" recorded by the apostle Paul in Galatians 5:19-21? Do you realize that almost 87% (13 out of 15) of the sinful deeds of the flesh are *relational* sins? That means a vast majority of our sinful behaviors are directly related in one way or another to our relationships with other people. Sexual immorality, impurity, sensuality, and orgies all involve other people. Enmity, strife, jealousy, fits of anger, rivalries, dissensions, divisions, and envy are all directed toward human objects. And as we have already noted, drunkenness almost always has a human counterpart destroyed somewhere in its wake. According to Jesus, the sins that come from the heart are also other-people orientated: "Evil thoughts, murder, adultery, sexual immorality, theft, false witness, slander" (Matt 15:18).

One of the most relationally destructive weapons of the human body is the tongue. James described the tongue as a "fire, a world of unrighteousness" and "set on fire by hell" (James 3:6). It is a "restless evil, full of deadly poison" (Jas 3:8). The tongue is one of the most destructive weapons known to men, inflicting pain far deeper into the human psyche than any gun or knife ever could. It can ruin a reputation, wreck a marriage, crush a spirit, and split a church.

Because of sin, broken relationships are endemic not only in our culture but the church as well. People are looking for a fix. Many churches have attempted to address the problem by offering marriage

---

[171] Anti Alcohol, "Social Effects," http://anti-alcohol.wikidot.com/social-effects (accessed 10/12/2011).

seminars and parenting classes. Marriage counseling, in fact, has become a major part of the pastoral ministry both corporately and individually. Sermons often offer practical steps toward building better relationships with those that we love. But as preachers of the gospel, we must realize that every broken relationship is rooted in sin. If we do not address the root problem, we can only bring superficial healing. The presence of sin is a malignant power that erodes unity and intimacy. True reconciliation can never occur without repentance and confession. As ministers of the Word, we have the responsibility to bring people face to face with the mischief of sin in their broken relationships.

Our Relationship to God

Of all the evil that sin causes in our relationships with other people, nothing compares to what sin does to our relationship with God. This is the greatest and worst stigma of sin. Our sin affects our relationship to God. Sadly, for many, this is the least of their concerns, but it is certainly the most destructive and most evil consequence they will ultimately face. King David's sin of adultery and murder ruined numerous relationships all around him. It destroyed the relationship between Uriah and his wife. It affected the relationships between a king and his subjects. Moreover, it certainly would have decimated the parents of Uriah and Bathsheba. Yet for all the ruin David caused, he knew that nothing compared to what his sin did to God. In his great confessional, David lamented, "Against You, You only, have I sinned and done what is evil in Your sight" (Ps 51:4). Our sin affects God more than the best among us—the most godly among us—could ever imagine.

David's attention to this detail is very foreign to our way of thinking. Many times we can see the pain our sin causes other people. We can easily imagine the devastation that David's sin undoubtedly caused so many people. However, David's language that his transgression was against God—and God alone— is quite alien to our way of thinking (cf. Ps 51:4). Most often we are clueless and even careless in considering how our sin affects God. In some ways this is natural because the effects of our sin on other people are visible, but we cannot see the effects of our sin on God. Moreover, people often communicate the hurt we cause them. When we hurt others, they can be quick to let us know. Even though God *has* communicated the offense of our sin in His word, it is not always immediately conveyed to us in the moments of our transgression. Like David, we can go on living ostensibly oblivious for months or even years under His intense displeasure.

By asserting that sin affects God, we might conceivably collide with a doctrine in Classic Theism called impassibility. This word, which ultimately derives from the Scriptural assertion that God is immutable or unchangeable,[172] means that God is incapable of pain, suffering, or emotion. Classic Theism has taught that God is impassible—not subject to suffering, pain, or the ebb and flow of involuntary passions. In the words of the Westminster Confession of Faith, God is "without body, parts, or passions, immutable."[173] The ultimate question of "without passions" is whether God actually reacts to His creation in an emotional way. In asserting that God was impassible, the Puritans were preeminently concerned to declare that God was not a capricious Being with wild mood swings and that His purposes and plans are never subject to the whims of man. If that is what impassibility means, then I would affirm it in its entirety.

In today's vernacular, however, does a God "without passions" accurately reflect the Self-revelation of God in Scripture? If we are not careful, we might infect the doctrine of impassibility with more philosophical reasoning than Scriptural teaching. We need to clarify impassibility so that it is based solely on Scriptural teaching and not human reasoning. If we base impassibility on God's immutability, it means that His character and His purpose are unchanging. It does not mean that God is incapable of passions (or emotions), or that His passions cannot be affected by our actions. In fact, the Scripture asserts that God is not only a God of great passions, but that He does, in fact, react to His creation in an emotional way. Even though the Puritan Thomas Watson would have affirmed the doctrine of impassibility, in practice he was more conventional. He wrote, "Sin

---

[172] Num 23:19; Mal 3:6; Heb 13:8; Jas 1:17.
[173] http://www.reformed.org/documents/index.html?mainframe=http://www.reformed.org/documents/westminster_conf_of_faith.html, chp. 2, sec. 1 (accessed 4/01/2012).

must bring a person low because sin is the only thing God has an antipathy against."[174] Antipathy is the opposite of sympathy; it is a hatred, disgust, or disdain. As Watson further explained, "that which draws forth the keeness [sic] of God's hatred is sin."[175] Watson was very aware that according to Scripture, sin excites and arouses the emotions of God's hatred and wrath against the sinner. Sin causes God to hate the sinner.

In Leviticus 20:23 the Lord warned Israel, "And you shall not walk in the customs of the nation that I am driving out before you, for they did all these things, and therefore I detested them." God detested them *because* they committed wretched abominations. When Israel turned their hearts against the Lord and rebelled against Him, the prophet Hosea signified a similar reaction from the Lord. Hosea 9:15 says, "Every evil of theirs is in Gilgal; there I began to hate them..." According to Hosea, Gilgal became a geographical and chronological marker to indicate the moment when God's emotions were aroused to a point of hatred toward the elect nation. If we understand God's impassibility to mean that He is incapable of responding emotionally to the actions of His creatures, then we miss the entire drama of redemption.

A misunderstanding of divine impassibility can produce disturbing theological aberrations even within the Christian community. Today, impassibility is, perhaps unwittingly, tied more to the love of God than anything else. It is assumed that God's love for His creatures is immense, immovable, and unshakable. In essence, it is commonly assumed that God's love is impassible, incapable of degree or reaction to the behavior of people. More often than not, however, the love of God touted today has been extracted and isolated from the total being of God, resulting in an anemic, shallow form of sentimentality that no longer has a place for anger or hatred against sin. The mantra of our culture is "God still loves you no matter what."

Not long ago a popular song hit the Christian charts with opening lines which declared, "He's not mad at you; He's not disappointed; His grace

---

[174] Watson, Mischief of Sin, 17.
[175] Ibid.

is greater still, than all of your wrong choices; He is full of mercy and He is ever kind. Hear His invitation, His arms are open wide."[176] There is clearly here an underlying premise of impassibility in that God could not possibly be "mad" at someone's "wrong choices." But is it responsible, or more importantly, biblically accurate to tell a sinner that God is not mad at them? Again, does not this miss the whole point of the gospel of grace?

If you want to do an interesting word study, look up the word "kindle" in a concordance. Time and again you will see that sin *kindles* the wrath of God. Sin stokes, arouses, or sets on fire God's anger. When Israel murmured against the Lord in the wilderness, Numbers 11:1 says that "His anger was kindled." The anger of the Lord was "kindled" against Israel when they followed Baal of Peor (Num 25:3). The Psalmist warns, "Kiss the Son, lest he be angry, and you perish in the way, for his wrath is quickly kindled." Since this is a Messianic Psalm, it is striking to consider that the Psalmist declares that the wrath of Jesus is "quickly kindled." Clearly, God is not a God without passions; and nothing arouses His wrath against the sinner but sin.

One of the perennial questions of life is why does God allow the wicked to sin with seeming impunity. Why does He allow the wicked to prosper when they sin with such a high hand against Him? The answer in Scripture is so apparent that it is scary. God lets men increase their sin so that He may increase His wrath and hatred and judgment against them. He lets them multiply their sin against Him so that He can multiply His wrath against them. For example, Abraham could not inherit the land because the iniquity of the Amorite was not yet complete (Gen 15:16). This implies that the increase in Amorite sin would ultimately propel God to drive them from their land. According to the Psalmist, the prosperity of the wicked puts them in a slippery place to make them fall to their ruin (Ps 73:18). And as Paul said, "Because of your hard and impenitent heart you are storing up wrath for yourself on the day of wrath…" (Rom 2:5).

---

[176] "Come as You Are" written by: Farren, Michael, Cates, Chad., Wood, Tony; Lyrics ©Warner/Chappell Music, Inc., Sony/ATV Music Publishing LLC

It is vitally important that preachers convey even to believers that sin affects their relationship to God. When David committed adultery and murder, 2 Samuel 11:27 said that what David did "displeased the Lord." God was not impassible towards David's sin, and He is not impassible towards ours. Paul warned believers to judge themselves when they participate in the Lord's Supper; otherwise they invite the Lord's judgment on themselves (1 Cor 11:28-32). The idea that a person can profess Christ and yet live however they please is anathema to the teaching found in the Bible. The author of Hebrews warns that sin in a life of believer incites God to discipline His own (Heb 12:4-11). Once a person comes to experience the trauma of their sin, how it draws forth the keenness of God's wrath and displeasure, they are ready for the conclusion of the matter. And for that you must turn to the next chapter.

> *To me it is profoundly liberating to recognize that all our troubles are ultimately rooted in one little word—sin.*
> Page 150

Conclusion - The Gospel and Sin

"So what is your book about?" I cannot count the number of times I was asked this question throughout the course of my writing. Several times I was surprised by the responses to my answer. When I answered "Sin" to an inquisitive unbeliever, her response was, "Oh, couldn't you just interview people in prison if you want to know the consequences of sin?" Honestly, I was a little flabbergasted at her suggestion; that thought had never even crossed my mind. When I began to think about the subject of sin, it was not other people's sin or even flagrant sins like murder or rape that prompted my interest. It was my sin, our secret sins, the subtle sins that blind us from even seeing sin. I knew I could write about sin because *I* am an expert on the subject already. I don't have to go to prisons for interviews; I can interview myself. Her response, however, is fairly indicative of what the world thinks about sin. Criminals, prostitutes, and drug dealers commit sin. The world can see sin in others, just never in themselves. When they think of sin they think of armed robbery or genocide; but they never think about self-righteousness, ingratitude, discontentment, pride, anxiety, or covetousness. In the words of Jerry Bridges, these are the "respectable sins" that we tolerate.[177]

On another occasion a believer responded to my answer more facetiously than serious. She said, "Oh, I wouldn't want to read that; it sounds so depressing." Again, I really wasn't prepared for that response, even though it was facetious. I guess the subject of sin is depressing. I knew from the beginning that a book about sin wouldn't be a bestseller. However, the thought never occurred to me that this subject was depressing. In fact, quite to the contrary, I found this subject absolutely liberating. We live in a world that is so messed up. You see it in the news. You see it in our families and schools. You see it in our churches. We see it in ourselves. People are running around looking for answers. They make appointments with shrinks who reassure them that their problem isn't their fault. Others (many others,

---

[177] Jerry Bridges, *Respectable Sins: Confronting the Sins We Tolerate* (Colorado Springs: NavPress, 2007).

in fact) try to fix their problems by swallowing pills to the tune of several billion dollars a year in America alone.[178] All this searching for answers and yet nothing changes. To me *that* is depressing. The fact is, people know something is wrong; but the answers they get are so complicated, so convoluted, and so futile.

To me it is profoundly liberating to recognize that all our troubles are ultimately rooted in one little word—sin. It is liberating because there is a remedy for it. It is astonishing that there is so much reluctance to accept this diagnosis. Obviously, anybody would be happy if they could put the blame for their problems on someone else; but many people would prefer to believe there is something wrong with their brain rather than their soul. Ironically, even the reluctance to admit our problem is rooted in sin. In our souls indwells an evil entity that hates to be exposed. Sin hides itself in the darkness of our heart. It disguises itself so it looks like something or someone else. Sin is more than happy to go to church as long as it is entertained; but it hates the light. When sin is uncovered it gets extremely agitated, because in the light sin is very ugly.

The Bible is not so reluctant to talk about sin. In fact, out of all the religious literature ever written in the whole world, I know of no corpus of writing that even comes close to addressing the problem of sin like the Bible. As a book, it is absolutely unique in that sin is central to its storyline: sin is what separated us from God in the first place (Gen 2:17). Sin needed the Law to be exposed (Rom 7:7–11). Sin necessitated the sacrificial system (Exod 29:36). Sin requires a blood sacrifice (Lev 4:20; Heb 9:22). Sin is what Israel did against God repeatedly (Jer 3:25). Sin is what the prophets constantly confronted in Israel (2 Chron 36:15; Jer 35:15). Sin is what we all do

---

[178] A recent article in Fox News reported that 20% of Americans use psychiatric drugs. The same article stated that in 2010, "Americans spent $16.1 billion on antipsychotics to treat depression, bipolar disorder and schizophrenia, $11.6 billion on antidepressants and $7.2 billion on treatment for ADHD, according to IMS Health, which tracks prescription drug sales." Fox News, "One in Five American Adults Takes Psychiatric Drugs," http://www.foxnews.com/health/2011/11/17/one-in-five-american-adults-takes-psychiatric-drugs/ (accessed 1/24/12).

(Rom 3:23). Sin is why Jesus Christ came into the world (1 Tim 1:15). Sin is what God is going to finally judge in the lake of fire (Rev 20:11-15). The conclusion should be obvious. If a man is going to assume the office of preaching, the subject of sin can never be far from his lips. John Owen wrote, "Let me add this to those who are preachers of the word, or intend, through the good hand of God, that employment: It is their duty to plead with men about their sins..."[179] More recently, Karl Menninger wrote, "The clergyman cannot minimize sin and maintain his proper role in our culture."[180]

The Cross of Christ

This book is written to awaken in preachers their duty to recapture the stigma of sin in their preaching to a generation in which sin abounds but truth about it does not. Such a ministry will always be relevant because sin is the all-encompassing problem men face every day of their life. The seriousness of sin and our focus on it do not find its ultimate locus in man, however. We must take sin seriously because God does. Stott wrote, "Nothing reveals the gravity of sin like the cross."[181] Although the cross has become a beautiful symbol of our faith, in the 1st century it was an emblem of shame and barbarism. In civilized societies where capital punishment is still practiced, attempts are made to retain the human dignity of the criminal even to the end. When the sentence is finally carried out, it is administered primarily by lethal injection to bring death as quickly and painlessly as possible. The intention of crucifixion was the exact opposite. The cross meant public humiliation and shame, and it was designed to maximize pain and prolong the dying experience. Stott described a typical Roman crucifixion:

> The prisoner would first be publicly humiliated by being stripped naked. He was then laid on his back on the ground, while his hands were either nailed or roped to the horizontal wooden beam (the *patibulum*), and his feet to the vertical pole. The cross was then

---

[179] Owen, *Overcoming Sin*, 84.
[180] Menninger, *Whatever Became of Sin?*, 198.
[181] Stott, *The Cross of Christ*, 83.

hoisted to an upright position and dropped into a socket which had been dug for it in the ground. Usually a peg or rudimentary seat was provided to take some of the weight of the victim's body and prevent it from being torn loose. But there he would hang, helplessly exposed to intense physical pain, daytime heat and night time cold. The torture would last several days.[182]

If it is only by this way that the demands of God's justice could be met, then sin must be serious indeed. John Piper wrote, "The cross stands in witness to the infinite worth of God and infinite outrage of sin."[183]

The crucifixion of the Lord Jesus Christ is no mere footnote to human history. It is, in fact, the culmination of history as the whole story of redemption marched to and flows from this very point. The author of Hebrews wrote, "But as it is, he has appeared once for all at the end (Greek *sunteleia*) of the ages to put away sin by the sacrifice of himself" (Heb 9:26). The emphasis on the cross is found throughout the New Testament.

The Centrality of the Cross in Christ's Ministry

The cross was central to Jesus' mission. Stott wrote, "What dominated his mind was not the living but the giving of his life."[184] Christ taught His disciples that the cross was a determinative force to His ministry. In Mark, Jesus speaks of His death as being unavoidable saying, "And he began to teach them that the Son of Man must (Greek *dei*) suffer many things and be rejected by the elders and the chief priests and the scribes and be killed, and after three days rise again. And he said this plainly" (Mark 8:31–2). During the height of His popularity as many were being healed, Christ gave this sobering reminder to His disciples, "Let these words sink into your ears: The Son of Man is about to be delivered into the hands of men" (Luke 9:44). As the days drew near to His suffering, Luke records His steadfast resolve saying, "He set His

---

[182] Ibid., 48.

[183] Piper, *The Supremacy of God in Preaching*, 32.

[184] Stott, *The Cross of Christ*, 32.

face to go to Jerusalem" (Luke 9:51). On the night of His betrayal, Luke records the institution of the Lord's Supper, in which the disciples are commanded to remember His death (Luke 22:19). And when the hour arrived and the weight of the moment hung on Him the heaviest, John records His resignation and recognition of His ultimate mission. Jesus prayed, "Now is My soul troubled. And what shall I say? Father, save Me from this hour? *But for this purpose I have come to this hour*" (John 12:27) [emphasis added].

The Centrality of the Cross in Paul's Ministry

Nothing defined the ministry and message of the apostle Paul like the cross. Though exalted to be an apostle, privileged to have seen the risen Christ "as one untimely born" (1 Cor 15:8), and receiver of heavenly visions (2 Cor 12:2–7), Paul declared, "But far be it from me to boast except in the cross of our Lord Jesus Christ" (Gal 6:14). The gospel that he preached was the "word of the cross" (1 Cor 1:18); and though it was foolish and offensive, he was determined that he would "preach Christ crucified" (1 Cor 1:23). It was the cross that reconciled God with men (Col 1:20); indeed, the message of the cross was the "power of God to salvation" (Rom 1:16). Paul was so confident in the supernatural power of this message that he devoted all of his preaching to it (1 Cor 2:2), and he eschewed any method of delivery that might in any way detract from its unique power (1 Cor 2:1-4).

The Gospel Remedy

If we look at the examples of Jesus and Paul, we conclude that the importance of a cross-centered ministry cannot be overstated. Stott wrote, "If the cross is not central to our religion, ours is not the religion of Jesus."[185] The cross is why we must take sin seriously. Men must come to see the problem of their sin so that they may come to find the remedy in the gospel. It is significant to see how the gospel uniquely addresses the problem of sin.

---

[185] Stott, *The Cross of Christ*, 68.

Repentance

The recognition of sin is so vital because of the gospel call to repentance. Throughout the New Testament repentance is recognized as a prerequisite of salvation. John the Baptist came preaching, "Repent, for the kingdom of heaven is at hand" (Matt 3:2; cf Mark 1:4). When Jesus began His earthly ministry, His sermons retained the same emphasis on repentance. Matthew says, "From that time Jesus began to preach, saying, 'Repent, for the kingdom of heaven is at hand'" (Matt 4:17; cf Mark 1:15). Moreover, He denounced those who did not repent (Matt 11:20; 12:38-42). Jesus also proclaimed that the repentance of a sinner brought joy to heaven (Luke 15:7; 10).

The message of repentance is a unifying theme to the preaching that we encounter in the New Testament. Just as Jesus retained John's emphasis on repentance, so too Jesus trained His twelve disciples in this model of preaching. Mark 6:12 says, "So they went out and proclaimed that people should repent." This model of preaching repentance was codified by the resurrected Lord when He commissioned His followers before His ascension. Luke 24:45-47 says,

> Then he opened their minds to understand the Scriptures, and said to them, "Thus it is written, that the Christ should suffer and on the third day rise from the dead, *and that repentance and forgiveness of sins should be proclaimed in his name to all nations*, beginning from Jerusalem." [emphasis added]

It is not surprising, therefore, that these disciples, who became the apostles of the church, retained the message of repentance.

The church originated and increased by the message of repentance. At Pentecost Peter preached repentance (Acts 2:38), and later as Gentiles were added to the fold, their conversion was deemed a "repentance that leads to life" (Acts 11:18). When the apostle Paul addressed the Greek philosophers in Athens, he declared that God "commands all people everywhere to repent" (Acts 17:30). Furthermore, when Paul met with the elders of the Ephesian church, he described his ministry as "testifying both to the Jews and Greeks of repentance towards God and of faith in our Lord Jesus Christ" (Acts 20:21; cf. 26:20). The apostle Peter explained the delay of Christ's Second coming as God's patience, "not wishing that any should perish, but that all should reach repentance" (2 Pet 3:9). Thus, the New Testament underscores the significance of repentance in the matter of salvation.

Historically, the church has always recognized the need of repentance. In the *Institutes of the Christian Religion,* John Calvin wrote, "The sum of the Gospel [sic] is, not without good reason, made to consist in repentance and the forgiveness of sins; and, therefore, where these two heads are omitted, any discussion concerning faith will be meager and defective, and indeed almost useless."[186] In a culture that has lost the language of sin, it is not surprising that the need for repentance also has been marginalized, if not outright rejected. In his book, *Absolutely Free,* Zane Hodges wrote, "Faith alone (not repentance *and* faith) is the sole condition for justification and eternal life" [emphasis his].[187] In this scheme, repentance is not the turning away from sin, but rather becomes a synonymous term to faith. Robert Wilkin wrote,

> Turning from sins is not a condition of eternal salvation. Is repentance in some sense a condition of eternal salvation? I believe that it is, but only in a few NT passages. In those texts a change of mind about Jesus Christ is given as a condition for eternal life. Changing one's mind about Christ is another way of speaking about believing in Him. Repentance is not a second condition for eternal salvation. It is another way of talking about faith in Christ.[188]

In this understanding, the preaching of repentance from sin is considered a work, and thus, has no part in the gospel. This view,

---

[186] John Calvin, *Institutes of Christian Religion*, trans. by Henry Beveridge, Esq. (London: Bonham Norton, 1599) Christian Classics Ethereal Library, 509 http://www.ccel.org/c/calvin/institutes/institutes.html [accessed September 20, 2011].

[187] Zane Hodges, *Absolutely Free: A Biblical Reply to Lordship Salvation* (Grand Rapids: Zondervan Publishing, 1989), 144.

[188] Robert Wilkin, "How to Communicate the Doctrine of Repentance Clearly," *Journal of the Grace Evangelical Society* 4, no. 1 (Autumn 1991): 47.

which has become known as "free grace," has gained widespread acceptance in the evangelical community.

Divorcing repentance of sin from the gospel has been disastrous to the evangelical church. We should not be surprised that the church in 21st century America looks a lot like the world. This faulty understanding of the nature of saving faith has bred a multitude of professing believers who remain "lovers of self, lovers of money, proud, arrogant, abusive, disobedient to their parents, ungrateful, unholy, heartless, unappeasable, slanderous, without self-control, brutal, not loving good, treacherous, reckless, swollen with deceit, lovers of pleasure rather than the lovers of God, having the appearance of godliness, but denying its power" (2 Tim 3:2–5). The apostle Paul said, "Avoid such people" (2 Tim 3:5). Calvin was right, when repentance is divorced from faith, "Any discussion concerning faith will be meager and defective, and indeed almost useless."[189]

The Forgiveness of Sin

The great promise of the gospel is the forgiveness of sin. We must expose sin because men must know what their problem is before the remedy can be applied. One of the most remarkable features of Christ's earthly ministry was the intentional discrimination against the self-righteous. I know that to modern sensibilities "discrimination" is a harsh word, but I believe it accurately describes the treatment the self-righteous received from Christ. Jesus said, "I came not to call the righteous, but sinners" (Mark 2:17; cf Matt 9:13; Luke 5:32). These were not idle words but rather a philosophy that governed His entire ministry. Jesus sought out sinners to the extent that His *enemies* called Him "a friend of tax collectors and sinners" (Matt 11:19).

As a historian of Jesus and the Church, Luke clearly recognized this as a distinguishing trait of Christ's ministry. Highlighting its importance, both Mark and Luke place the saying "I did not come to call the righteous" at the beginning of Christ's ministry (Mark 2:17; Luke 5:32). Luke, however, seems to develop this theme in more detail. He

---

[189] Calvin, *Institutes,* Book Third, chp. 3, sec. 1, 509.

records numerous encounters of repentance (several which are unique to his Gospel) in people who were deemed great sinners by society. On two occasions these "sinners" are, ironically, held up by Jesus as a paradigm of the way which is right.

The first is a woman who interrupts Jesus' dinner in the home of a Pharisee. Luke describes her as "a woman of the city, a sinner" (Luke 7:37). This is a brazen act, but it does not flow from a proud heart. Luke records that this woman was "standing behind Him at His feet, weeping, she began to wet his feet with her tears and wiped them with the hair of her head and kissed His feet and anointed them with the ointment" (Luke 7:38). Obviously such a scene attracted the attention of the Pharisee, and his response was revealing. He said to himself, "If this man were a prophet, he would have known who and what sort of woman this is who is touching him, for she is a sinner" (Luke 7:39). In his reasoning we learn that the reputation (perhaps even occupation) of this woman was very obvious. Moreover, if Jesus were a prophet, he surmised, Jesus would know what sort of woman this was—even if He had never met her personally. More importantly, the implication was that if Jesus knew what sort of woman this was, He would stop her. Jesus, however, did not stop her; instead, she becomes a lesson for the way that is right. Jesus said,

> Do you see this woman? I entered your house; you gave me no water for my feet, but she has wet my feet with her tears and wiped them with her hair. You gave me no kiss, but from the time I came in she has not ceased to kiss my feet. You did not anoint my head with oil, but she has anointed my feet with ointment. Therefore I tell you, her sins, which are many, are forgiven- for she loved much. But he who is forgiven little, loves little. And he said to her, "Your sins are forgiven." (Luke 7:44–8).

The self-righteous one is rebuked, while the brokenhearted sinner receives forgiveness.

The second example comes from a parable of Jesus. Luke is careful to put this parable in context. He writes, "He also told this parable to some who trusted in themselves that they were righteous, and treated others with contempt" (Luke 18:9). Though an invented story, this parable produces a powerfully vivid image of two men who are praying in the temple, one a Pharisee, the other a tax collector. The men are in eye sight of each other. The Pharisee prays first, "God, I thank you that I am not like other men, extortioners, unjust, adulterers, or even like this tax collector" (Luke 18:11). You get the distinct impression that his eyes are fixed on the heavens, except for a brief glance towards the lowlife over yonder. His self-righteousness is palpable as he recounts his achievements, "I fast twice a week. I give tithes of all that I get" (Luke 18:12). Before the tax collector prays, however, Jesus describes his posture. "But the tax collector, standing afar off, would not even lift his eyes toward heaven, but beat his breast..." (Luke 18:13). This man is embarrassed and unworthy to stand before God. He cannot even look up. From the perspective of a 1st century Jew, the tax collector should have been embarrassed. He was the lowest of the low. The publican's prayer is short and probably quiet: "God, be merciful to me, a sinner." The contrast could not be starker. A 1st century Jew would have viewed the Pharisee as the paradigm of righteousness and the tax collector as a paradigm of disgust. However, in Jesus' parable, the convicted sinner becomes an example for the way that is right. Jesus said, "I tell you, this man went down to his house justified, rather than the other" (Luke 18:14).

In both of these instances, the internal awareness of sin is highlighted. All men are sinners, but not all men feel the weight of their sin. Both of these individuals did, and the realization of their sin was psychologically traumatizing. One wept, the other beat his breast. In an age that views psychological trauma as something to be avoided at all cost, it is almost incomprehensible that Jesus would lift them up as a lesson in what is right. Yet, Jesus only illustrated what God had made known long ago:

> Psalm 51:17—The sacrifices of God are a broken spirit; a broken and contrite heart, O God, you will not despise.
>
> Psalm 147:3—He heals the brokenhearted and binds up their wounds.
>
> Isaiah 57:15—For thus says the One who is high and lifted up, who inhabits eternity, whose name is Holy: "I dwell in the high and holy place, and also with him who is of a contrite and

> lowly spirit, to revive the spirit of the lowly, and to revive the heart of the contrite."
>
> Isaiah 61:1—The Spirit of the Lord GOD is upon me, because the LORD has anointed me to bring good news to the poor; he has sent me to bind up the brokenhearted.
>
> Isaiah 66:2—But this is the one to whom I will look: he who is humble and contrite in spirit and trembles at my word.

The awareness of sin brings the guilt that traumatizes the soul. The lesson to be learned is that guilt is a necessary and appropriate response to sin. God does not despise those who are traumatized by their sin. Instead, He offers to them the gospel to heal their brokenness. The Good News is that because of Jesus Christ and His work, we can be completely forgiven of all sin. From a biblical perspective, much of what we consider to be depression today is guilt. Sadly, men devise elaborate schemes to assuage or alleviate that guilt without repentance and the forgiveness of sins.

Gospel-Centered Preaching

The gospel is the treasure of the church and the heart of Christianity. Indeed, Paul understood the gospel as something which God Himself had entrusted to him (1 Tim 1:11). It is no wonder, then, that when Paul spoke of the gospel, he made some audacious claims. Today, the church of Jesus Christ needs to take a fresh look at those claims and determine whether we believe them or not. One passage that needs fresh attention is 1 Corinthians 15:1–4.

> Now I would remind you, brothers, of the gospel I preached to you, which you received, in which you stand, and by which you are being saved, if you hold fast to the word I preached to you—unless you believed in vain. *For I delivered to you as of first importance what I also received*: that Christ died for our sins in accordance with the Scriptures, that he was buried, that he was raised on the third day in accordance with the Scriptures [emphasis added].

One of the most remarkable things about this passage in chapter 15 is that it comes after chapters 14, 13, 12, 11, and so on. Paul addressed some heavy issues in this letter, like church unity, church discipline, sexual immorality, and marriage and divorce. These are major issues even today; yet in chapter 15 Paul comes back to make it clear that the gospel is of "first importance." The other issues are clearly important, but none on the level of the gospel. Amidst all the issues in the Corinthian church, Paul brought them back to the supremacy of the gospel.

The supremacy of the gospel was central to Paul's ministry. In fact, in the second chapter of this epistle Paul said, "For I decided to know nothing among you except Jesus Christ and him crucified" (1 Cor 2:2). Obviously that cannot mean that other issues would not be addressed. What it must mean is that the gospel encompasses every issue that needs to be addressed. Paul's ministry was gospel-centered. If people visit our church, what would they perceive to be of "first importance" to us? It is easy to give lip service to the gospel. I am convinced that one of the most significant errors in American evangelicalism is that we *assume* the gospel. We assume people already know it, believe, and implement it in their lives. It is a fatal assumption. We need to consider what a gospel-centered ministry looks like. The implementation of a gospel-centered ministry would result in significant changes.

Many sincere Christians believe that a gospel-centered ministry would be fulfilled by tacking on a gospel invitation at the end of a sermon. This is a common practice in many churches today. However, I would suggest that such a practice is actually *antithetical* to a gospel-centered ministry. Calling unbelievers to repentance and faith is clearly a part of the gospel presentation. But tacking on an invitation at the end of a sermon immediately provokes a dichotomy within the congregation in which the believer is allowed to check out. The believer thinks, "This isn't for me. This is for the unbelievers. I have already believed the gospel." This attitude fundamentally misses the importance of Paul's determination to preach the gospel. He said, "For I decided to know *nothing among you* except Jesus Christ and Him crucified" (1 Cor 2:2) [emphasis added]. Paul was determined to preach the gospel to *believers*. Once you understand the importance of the gospel to the believer, it will change the way you view salvation.

The evangelical culture of our day primarily views salvation as a one-time event. People say a prayer and get saved. Paul had a different view of salvation. Listen to how Paul addresses the Corinthians, "Now I would remind you, brothers, of the gospel I preached to you, which you received, in which you stand, and *by which you are being saved*" (1 Cor 15:1–2). In the word "saved" Paul employed a present passive verb (Greek *sōdzesthe*) that indicates continuing action. We have not just been saved, but we are, in fact, in the process of being saved. How do we continue in the process of salvation? Paul answers, "If you hold fast to the word I preached to you—unless you believed in vain" (1 Cor 15:2). The gospel is something that believers have to "hold fast to." A faith that does not hold fast to the gospel is a vain or futile faith (I Cor 15:2). Paul raises the sobering possibility that a person who begins to believe, may, in fact, not continue to believe. Modern evangelicals do not think that way. If you do, it changes the way you view salvation.[190] Belief in the gospel needs to be continually renewed and implemented throughout our life.

If the way you view salvation changes, it will change how you live the Christian life. In 1 Corinthians 15:1 Paul speaks of the gospel as that "in which you stand." The believer never moves from the gospel; he stands in it. No matter where we are or how much we have grown as a Christian, we always remain trusting in our perfect Substitute. Standing in the gospel addresses two of the most fundamental problems in the Christian life: sin and trials. Sin is a perennial problem even for the believer. Many Christians fail to understand that progressive sanctification can be "horrifically slow."[191] Looking at

---

[190] This brings up the subject of eternal security, a subject beyond the scope of this work. The view of salvation presented in this chapter will raise serious questions about the common mantra "once saved, always saved." However, the view presented is in accordance to the Reformed understanding of the perseverance of the saints, whereby truly regenerated saints will persevere to the end.

[191] I got this phrase from an excellent sermon by Matt Chandler entitled "Blessings and Woes" preached on Feb. 17, 2008.
http://www.thevillagechurch.net/media/sermons/transcripts/200802171100HVW
C21ASAAA_MattChandler_LukePt14-BlessingsAndWoes.pdf (accessed 2/1/12).

salvation only as a past event creates untold misery and desperation in myriads of Christians. Modern evangelicalism has largely presented the gospel as something that the unbeliever needs and the believer has already received. Salvation as a one time event says, "Believe in Jesus and you are saved." Maybe everything is wonderful *for a while*; but then the struggles come. Sin rears its ugly head, and Christians begin to wonder what is wrong with them. They begin to despair because they thought they were saved. No one told them that the gospel not only saved them, but it *keeps* them saved. Paul said, "To us *who are being saved*," the word of the cross, "*is* the power of God" (1 Cor 1:18) [emphasis added]. The believer stands in the gospel. Gospel-centered preaching reminds the believer that the gospel is the remedy for the ongoing struggle against sin. Others who have faced these struggles with sin but never learned to rely on the gospel come to a chilling conclusion: "I tried Jesus. He didn't work."

Gospel-centered preaching is also preeminently important in the matter of trials and suffering. During his missionary travels, Paul returned to the city of Antioch, "strengthening the souls of the disciples, encouraging them to continue in the faith, and *saying that through many tribulations we must enter the kingdom of God*" (Acts 14:22) [emphasis added]. We are destined to encounter many trials and tribulations in this life. The gospel is the anchor to our soul. It is the only sure foundation on which we can stand when the winds of persecution and trouble blow hard. Trials have an incredible ability to shake our faith. They can cause us to doubt God's love or concern for us. Gospel-centered preaching equips believers for suffering by continually pointing them to the cross, which is God's grand demonstration of love towards us. One of the most glorious examples of gospel-centered preaching is found in Paul's letter to the Christians in Rome. He wrote,

> What then shall we say to these things? If God is for us, who can be against us? He who did not spare his own Son but gave him up for us all, how will he not also with him graciously give us all things? Who shall bring any charge against God's elect? It is God who justifies. Who is to condemn? Christ Jesus is the one who died- more than that, who was raised- who is at the right hand of God, who indeed is interceding for us. Who shall separate us

from the love of Christ? Shall tribulation, or distress, or persecution, or famine, or nakedness, or danger, or sword? As it is written, "For your sake we are being killed all the day long; we are regarded as sheep to be slaughtered." No, in all these things we are more than conquerors through him who loved us. For I am sure that neither death nor life, nor angels nor rulers, nor things present nor things to come, nor powers, nor height nor depth, nor anything else in all creation, will be able to separate us from the love of God in Christ Jesus our Lord. (Rom 8:31–9).

Christian preacher, the problem of sin and suffering is all around us. The world searches in vain for answers. But to us has been committed "the glorious gospel of the blessed God" (1 Tim 1:11).

A Preaching Paradigm

John Owen believed it was the preacher's duty to plead with men about their sin.[192] But what does a preaching ministry like this look like today? Here in the Midwest, a Baptist pastor garnered national attention by protesting at military funerals with signs containing vile slogans particularly against homosexuals. Is that what preaching against sin must look like? Not at all. This man doesn't plead with men about their sin. He denounced sinners. I do not think that railing against sin or a return to the caricatured "hellfire and brimstone" genre is probable or necessary. Let me suggest several important components of this kind of preaching:

Be Faithful to the Word

The duty to plead with men about their sin did not originate with Owen. Paul instructed Timothy to "Preach the word; be ready in season and out of season; *reprove, rebuke,* and exhort with complete patience and teaching" (2 Tim 4:2) [emphasis added]. Today, the pastor is under a lot of pressure to keep his sermons positive and encouraging. While edification is clearly part of the pastoral ministry (Eph 4:12), it seems significant to me that, according to 2 Timothy 4:2, preaching the Word and reproofs are intentionally arranged in tandem:

---

[192]Owen, *Overcoming Sin*, 84.

reproofs follow preaching the Word. In the constancy of preaching, reproofs are a necessary component to the ministry if one is going to be a faithful expositor of the Word. A pastor does not always have to try to intentionally speak about sin; however, he must be intentional in expositing the whole counsel of God's Word (Acts 20:27). A systematic exposition of the whole of Scripture provides a varied diet for the congregation and ensures that Scripture, not the pastor, establishes the subject matter. It also ensures that sin in all its facets and manifestations will be dealt with. Preaching this way honors the primacy of God's Word and keeps pastors from camping on their pet peeves.

In the course of the faithful proclamation of inspired truth, men will always be confronted with the divine standard of which we all fall short. It is the ethical imperatives of Scripture that bring the knowledge of sin. Paul said in Romans 3:20, "Through the law comes knowledge of sin." In his commentary on the Sermon on the Mount, Carson made this humble admission, "The more I read these chapters—Matthew 5, 6, and 7—the more I am both drawn to them and *shamed* by them" [emphasis added].[193] I do not believe this is an exceptional response, but rather a very normal and appropriate response to the faithful ministry of the Word. If we are going to recover the stigma of sin, the first order of business is to be faithful expositors of Scripture.

Be Compassionate

How we address the subject of sin is very important. Those who rail against sin often fail to convey an appropriate attitude towards those who sin. Our great High Priest is able to "sympathize with our weaknesses" (Heb 4:15). In fact, in order to perfectly qualify as our Mediator, Christ was "one who in every respect has been tempted as we are" (Heb 4:15). Christ is able to sympathize with our weaknesses because in His flesh He experienced our weaknesses. This sympathy was expected of Israel's high priests because as Hebrews 5:2 states,

---

[193] D.A. Carson, *Jesus' Sermon on the Mount and His Confrontation with the Word* (Grand Rapids: BakerBooks, 1987), 11.

"He [the earthly high priest] can deal gently with the ignorant and wayward, since he himself is beset with weakness." If our perfect Savior is able to sympathize with sinners, how much more should imperfect ministers demonstrate compassion to those to whom they preach? Al Mohler wrote, "True compassion demands speaking the truth in love—and there is the problem. Far too often, our courage is more evident than our compassion."[194]

One of Paul's most frequent admonitions in dealing with the obstinate and sinful was to be gentle, an attitude that flows out of compassion. He modeled this in his own ministry. He entreated the erring Corinthians "by the meekness and gentleness of Christ" (2 Cor 10:1). Likewise, Timothy was to correct his opponents in gentleness (2 Tim 2:25). Paul urged those who sought to restore one caught in any transgression to do so "in a spirit of gentleness" (Gal 6:1). Titus was commanded to "be gentle, and show perfect courtesy toward all people" (Titus 3:2). And where would this gentle spirit come from? Paul stated that it should flow from our experience of our own fallen nature. He wrote in the following verse: "For we ourselves were once foolish, disobedient, led astray, slaves to various passions and pleasures, passing our days in malice and envy, hated by others and hating one another" (Titus 3:3). When dealing with people of corrupted wills, deceived hearts, blinded eyes, or relationship-destroying sins, the preacher should have a wealth of personal experience with the same from which to draw forth deep compassion for those to whom he minsters.

Be Transparent

Many people assume that ministers have reached an uncommonly high spiritual state. It is true that pastors should be full of integrity (1 Tim 3:1-7), examples to the flock (1 Tim 4:12), and spiritually mature (1Tim 5:22); but pastors never arrive at a level when they cease struggling with sin. Pastors share in the same inward groaning of all believers, who wait for "the redemption of our bodies" (Rom 8:23).

---

[194] Al Mohler, "Courage and Compassion on Homosexuality," http://www.crosswalk.com/news/al-mohler/courage-and-compassion-on-homosexuality-1252946.html (accessed 4/3/2012).

The desires of pastor's flesh are still opposed to the desires of the Spirit (Gal 5:17). As I look back over my Christian life, my progress in sanctification has been slow. As a young man I yearned for a "second blessing"—a second work of grace that would result in total sanctification.[195] Yet the more I sought this "total sanctification," the more it seemed to elude me. No matter how much I surrendered or how hard I prayed, I still struggled with sin. A turning point came in my continued reading of Christian biographies. I vividly remember the encouraging dismay that came from the realization that many of these heroes of the faith were anything but perfect. They struggled in ways that were similar to my own. It was a transforming moment in my Christian development to realize that this side of heaven, I will never "arrive." It is only when Jesus returns that I and all of creation "will be set free from its bondage to decay and obtain the freedom of the glory of the children of God" (Rom 8:21).

I believe that when preachers deal with the subject of sin, they should be transparent with their own struggles. This can be a tremendous encouragement to the flock. As Paul wrote, "No temptation has overtaken you that is not common to man" (1 Cor 10:13). This followed the stark warning, "Let anyone who thinks that he stands take heed lest he fall (1 Cor 10:12). A preacher's transparency should lead to a compassionate humility as he pleads with other men about their sin. Every honest preacher will see with Paul that among sinners, he is "foremost" (1 Tim 1:15). And he will be able to say with Paul, "But I received mercy for this reason, that in me, as the foremost, Jesus Christ might display his perfect patience as an example to those who were to believe in him for eternal life" (1 Tim 1:16).

---

[195] Much of this influence came from reading books by Hudson Taylor, Amy Carmichael, and R.A. Torrey. They were involved in the Keswick Convention in the late 19th century that fostered the "Higher Life" movement. This movement stressed the need for full surrender to God which would lead to abundant power and victory in the Christian life.

Bibliography

Bibliography

Beck, James and Bruce Demarest. *The Human Person in Theology and Psychology*. Grand Rapids: Kregel Publications, 2005.

Bell, Rob. *Velvet Elvis: Repainting the Christian Faith*. Grand Rapids: Zondervan Publishing, 2005.

_____. *Love Wins: A Book About Heaven, Hell, and The Fate of Every Person Who Ever Lived*. New York: Harper One, 2011.

Berkhof, Louis. *Systematic Theology*. 1932. Reprint. Grand Rapids: Eerdmans Publishing, 1996.

Biddle, Mark. *Missing the Mark: Sin and Its Consequences in Biblical Theology*. Nashville: Abingdon Press, 2005.

Boice, James Montgomery and Philip Ryken. *The Doctrines of Grace: Rediscovering the Evangelical Gospel*. Wheaton: Crossway Books, 2002.

Bonar, Andrew. *Memoirs and Remains of the Rev. Robert Murray McCheyne*. Edinburgh: William Oliphant, 1874.

Bonhoeffer, Dietrich. *Life Together, The Classic Exploration of Christian Community*. New York: HarperOne, 1954.

Boston, Thomas, and David Young. *Human Nature in Its Fourfold State: Of Primitive Integrity, Entire Depravity, Begun Recovery, and Consummate Happiness Or Misery*. N.d., Reprint. Nabu Press, 2010.

Bridges, Jerry. *Respectable Sins: Confronting the Sins We Tolerate*. Colorado Springs, CO: NavPress, 2007.

Bulkley, Edward. *Why Christians Can't Trust Psychology*. Eugene, OR: Harvest House Publishers, 1993.

Burroughs, Jeremiah. *Evil of Evils, or the Exceeding Sinfulness of Sin*. 1654. Reprint. Ligonier, PA: Solio Deo Gloria Publications, 1992.

Calvin, John. *Institutes of Christian Religion*. Trans. by Henry Beveridge, Esq. London: Bonham Norton, 1599. Christian Classics Ethereal Library. November 1999. Calvin College. http://www.ccel.org/c/calvin/institutes/institutes.html [accessed September 20, 2001].

Carson, D.A. *Jesus' Sermon on the Mount and His Confrontation with the World*. Grand Rapids: BakerBooks, 1987.

_____. *The Difficult Doctrine of the Love of God*. Wheaton: Crossway Books, 2000.

Chan, Francis and Preston Sprinkle. Erasing hell: what God said about eternity, and the *things we've made up*. Colorado Springs: David C. Cook, 2011.

Charnock, Stephen. *The Existence and Attributes of God.* 1853. Reprint. Grand Rapids: Baker Books, 1996.

Edwards, Jonathan. *Freedom of the Will.* Vancouver: Eremitical Press, 2009.

Erickson, Millard J. *The Postmodern World, Discerning the Time and the Spirit of Our Age.* Wheaton, IL: Crossway Books, 2002.

Harrison, Elliot. *The Bearing of Psychology upon Religion.* New York: Association Press, 1927.

Hodges, Zane. *Absolutely Free: A Biblical Reply to Lordship Salvation.* Dallas: Zondervan Publishing, 1989.

Hoekema, Anthony. *Created in God's Image.* Grand Rapids: Eerdmans Publishing, 1994.

Fanella, John J. *Sinners in the Hands of an Angry God, Made Easier to Read.* Phillipsburg, NJ: Whitaker House, 1996.

Ganz, Richard. *PsychoBabble: The Failure of Psychology and the Biblical Alternative.* Wheaton, IL: Crossway Books, 1993.

Grudem, Wayne. Making Sense of Man and Sin: One of Seven Parts from *Grudem's Systematic Theology*. Grand Rapids: Zondervan Publishing, 2011.

_____. *Systematic Theology*. Grand Rapids: Zondervan, 1994.

Kellemen, Robert. *Soul Physicians: A Theology of Soul Care and Spiritual Direction.* Taneytown, MD: RPM Books, 2005.

Kemp, Charles F. *Physicians of the Soul: A History of Pastoral Counseling.* New York: MacMillen, 1947.

Kimball, Dan. *The Emerging Church: Vintage Christianity for New Generations.* Grand Rapids: Zondervan Publishing, 2003.

Lloyd-Jones, Martyn David. *Spiritual Depression: Its Causes and Cure.* Grand Rapids: Eerdmans Publishing, 1965.

_____. *Studies in the Sermon on the Mount*. Grand Rapids: Eerdmans Publishing, 1976.

Luther, Martin. *Bondage of the Will.* Peabody, MA: Hendrickson Publishers, 2008.

MacArthur, Jr, John. *The Love of God.* Dallas: Word Publishing, 1996.

Mangis, Michael. *Signature Sins: Taming Our Wayward Hearts.* Downers Grove, IL: InterVarsity Press, 2008.

Mardsen, George M. *A Short Life of Jonathan Edwards*. Grand Rapids: Eerdmans Publishing, 2008.

Masters, Peter M. *Physicians of Souls*. London: Wakeman Trust, 2002.

McKnight, Scott. *A Community Called Atonement*. Nashville, TN: Abingdon Press, 2007.

McMinn, Mark R. *Sin and Grace in Christian Counseling: An Integrative Paradigm*. Downers Grove, IL: InterVarsity Press, 2008.

McLaren, Brian. *A Generous Orthodoxy*. Grand Rapids: Zondervan Publishing, 2004.

_____. *A New Kind of Christianity: Ten Questions that are Transforming the Faith*. New York: HarperCollins Publishers, 2010.

Menninger, Karl. *Whatever Became of Sin?* Westerleigh, UK: Hawthorn Books, 1973.

Nicholi, Armandi. *The Question of God, C.S. Lewis and Sigmund Freud Debate God, Love, Sex, and the Meaning of Life*. New York: Free Press, 2002.

Owen, John. Editors Kelly M. Kapic and Justin Taylor. *Overcoming Sin and Temptation*. Wheaton: Crossway Books, 2006.

_____. *The Mortification of Sin*. (N.p., n.d.).

Packer, J. I. *A Quest for Godliness: The Puritan Vision of the Christian Life*. Grand Rapids: Crossway Books, 1990.

Pagitt, Doug. *Preaching Re-Imagined, The Role of the Sermon in Communities of Faith*. Grand Rapids: Zondervan Publishing, 2005.

Piattelli-Palmarini, Massimo. *Inevitable Illusions: How Mistakes of Reason Rule Our Minds*. New York: John Wiley & Sons, 1994.

Piper, John. *The Supremacy of God in Preaching*. Grand Rapids: Baker Book, 1990.

_____. *When I Don't Desire God*. Wheaton, IL: Crossway Books, 2004.

Poe, Harry L. *See No Evil: The Existence of Sin in an Age of Relativism*. Grand Rapids: Kregel Publications, 2004.

Powlison, David. "What is Sin?," *The Journal of Biblical Counseling* 25, No. 2 (Spring 2007).

Powlison, David. *Seeing with New Eyes: Counseling and the Human Condition through the Lens of Scripture*. Phillipsburg, NJ: P&R Publishing Company, 2003.

Schuller, Robert. *Self-Esteem: The New Reformation*. Waco, TX: Word Books, 1982.

Shedd, William. *Dogmatic Theology.* 1888. Reprint. New York: C. Scribner's, N.d.

Shorter, Edward. *From Paralysis to Fatigue: A History of Psychosomatic Illness in the Modern Era.* New York: The Free Press, 1992.

Shuster, Marguerite. *The Fall and Sin: What We Have Become as Sinners.* Grand Rapids: Eerdmans Publishing, 2004.

Smith, Robert. *The Christian Counselor's Medical Desk Reference.* Stanley, NC: Timeless Texts, 2000.

Stanford, Matthew S. *The Biology of Sin.* Colorado Springs: Biblica Publishing, 2010.

John Stott. *The Cross of Christ.* Downers Grove, IL: Intervarsity Press, 1986.

Taylor, Barbara Brown. *Speaking of Sin: The Lost Language of Salvation.* Lanham, MD: Cowley Publications, 2000.

Tyler, David and Kurt Grady. *Deceptive Diagnosis: When Sin is Called Sickness.* Bemidji, MN: Focus Publishing, 2006.

Veith, Jr., Gene Edward. *Postmodern Times: A Christian Guide to Contemporary Thought and Culture.* Wheaton, IL: Crossway Books, 1994.

Venning, Ralph. *The Sinfulness of Sin.* 1669. Reprint. Carlisle, PA: Banner of Truth, 1993.

Warren, Rick. *The Purpose Driven Church.* Grand Rapids: Zondervan Publishing, 1995.

Watson, Thomas. *The Mischief of Sin.* 1671. Reprint. Morgan, PA: Soli Deo Gloria Publications, 1994.

_____. *The Doctrine of Repentance.* N.d.; Reprint. Carlisle, PA: The Banner of Truth, 2009.

Welch, Edward T., *Blame it on the Brain?: Distinguishing Chemical Imbalances, Brain Disorders, and Disobedience.* Phillipsburg, NJ: Presbyterian and Reformation Publishing, 1998.

Bock, Darrell. *Luke Volume 1: 1:-9:50.* BECNT. Grand Rapids: BakerBooks, 1994.

Davids, Peter. *Commentary on James.* NIGTC. Grand Rapids: Eerdmans Publishing, 1982.

Doriani, Daniel. *James.* REC. Phillipsburgh, NJ: P&R Publishing, 2007.

Hodge, Charles. *Commentary on the Epistle to the Romans.* Grand Rapids: Eerdmans Publishing, 1994.

_____. *Commentary on the First Epistle to the Corinthians.* Grand Rapids: Eerdmans Publishing, 1994.

Luther, Martin. *Commentary on Romans.* N.d. Reprint. Grand Rapids: Zondervan, 1954.

Moo, Douglas. *The Epistle to the Romans.* TNIC. Grand Rapids: Eerdmans Publishing, 1996.

Morris, Leon. *The Epistle to the Romans.* PNTC. Grand Rapids: Eerdmans Publishing, 1988.

O'Brien, Peter. *The Letter to the Ephesians.* PNTC. Grand Rapids: Eerdmans Publishing, 1999.

Schreiner, Thomas. *Romans.* BEC. Grand Rapids: Baker Academic, 1998.

Scroggie, H. Graham. *The Psalms.* Old Tappan: NJ, Fleming H. Revell Company, 1978.

Wilson, Gerald. *The NIV Application Commentary—Psalms Vol. 1.* Grand Rapids: Zondervan, 2002.

www.ingramcontent.com/pod-product-compliance
Lightning Source LLC
Chambersburg PA
CBHW061324040426
42444CB00011B/2768